The Wounded

THE
WOUNDED

Morality Tale

MICK MALONE

A Catalogue-in-Publication is available from
the National Library of Australia.

ISBN: 978-0-646-95477-6

eISBN: 978-0-646-95504-9

CONTENTS

OLD MATES

"CALL US AN AMBULANCE!"

"Call us an ambulance!"

Nick swept the eyes of his two bemused companions, they knew what was coming next. He stepped back towards the young Lebanese, last seen as an unconscious tangle of arms and legs on the bar room floor.

"OK Habibi, you're a fucking ambulance, now get the fuck out of my pub, before I hurt you, and take that fat sack of shit with you!"

With that, Nick placed one foot squarely on the testicles of the Adidas-clad, gold chain wearing, poor misunderstood refugee's still unconscious companion. He trod down heavily, pivoted and headed back to his drinking partners, Ray Salmon (Sockeye) and Ray Saunders (Pillows).

Pillows wiped tears of mirth from his seen-too-much eyes and chortled.

"That's a tired old joke Nick, but you get me every time, must be your delivery old son."

"You must be getting crotchety in your old age," from Sockeye, "that pirouette on his nuts ain't exactly your usual style".

"Well, true, not much point at the moment, but when muscles wakes up with a couple of aches of his own to think about, he might not be so keen to come back to the Castle."

The Windsor Castle, in tradition of all old Paddington pubs, had for years been owned by a succession of retired police sergeants. As everybody in Sydney town knew, there was no police corruption in the Premier Bob Askin days, so they must have paid for these million dollar inner city watering holes, with their wives' carefully husbanded shopping money.

The Windsor owed much of its own notoriety to the sixties. When the hippies came to Sydney and flower power stretched out to embrace a nation, it was to the Windsor they did come and from its doors did the gunja, speed and acid flow.

More than a few parental natives of today's Nimbin took his or her first drink at the bar of the Windsor Castle.

Property booms boomed, hippies became junkies, the TAB was born and crime commissions raised their ugly heads.

Many an eastern suburbs publican turned a wistful eye to Queensland.

 Owned by King Joh and run by Chancellor Russ, it was the perfect place for an old copper to put his feet up. A new generation of publicans appeared, sons of daddy's money who thought running a pub was easy living. They ripped out the tile walls, installed real kitchens and hired passable chefs.

The yuppie pub restaurant was born.

As the grandsons of the squattocracy discovered pub life wasn't all beer and bar maids, one by one they sold their holdings back to the appropriate owners. A new shift of retired sergeants assumed their appropriate functions. Sockeye was one of these.

He had earned his nickname both as an allusion to his surname and for his lightning-fast and ferocious habit of awarding broken noses and black eyes to almost every crook he brought in.

"Makes it easier to remember which ones are mine," he claimed.

"Just another vicious violent bloody copper," would joke his mate of thirty years Nick Fallon.

Sockeye met Saunders the day his now bar manager and permanent companion had his unfortunate nickname thrust upon him. They'd been assigned their first shift with the old twenty first division with a mandate to clean up the street gangs.

In good old Aussie fashion the street level counselling was accomplished with large groups of large coppers wearing large boots and carrying big sticks. Following their first encounter group, Pillows was found at the bottom of the pile of counselled street thugs, five heads resting peacefully on various parts of his anatomy. His twenty first brethren thought it a great joke, Pillows bit his tongue and wore it.

Nick had been sitting for an hour waiting for his old mates, and while prison education programs aren't quite the success some politicians may claim, Nick's twelve months in Long Bay jail had taught him patience and the habit of seeing and hearing everything within fifteen metres.

The pair at the pool table had caught his attention.

At first amused, then annoyed, then thoroughly pissed off, he watched them progress from sledging their way to a twenty dollar pool win, to a blatant, to Nick's eyes, pick pocket. At least they had the good sense to lose that game and hand their victim twenty dollars of his own money to stop him reaching for his now missing wallet. It was their third game that caused the steam to begin wafting from Nick's ears. A young lunching accounts executive had the temerity to complain about the mouth's verbal tactics, this gave muscles the excuse to grab him by the scruff of the neck and bang his head twice against the adjacent wall. He then fined the battered bean counter the contents of his wallet.

''For calling my brother a cheat!'' and pitched him out the door.

Nick shifted uneasily in his set and muttered.

'''Come on Sockeye, get here before I break the rules and do something for nothing.''

Luckily his old friend plus side kick chose that moment to make his entrance, Ray Salmon immediately spotted Nick. It was funny to see, his face lit up, clouded and lit again as he quickly considered the possible reasons for Nick's visit, then settled on the usually enjoyable mischief of his mate's presence.

"G'day mate" with a warm extended hand from Sockeye "where you been last coupla weeks, and what's with the suntan, haven't been out during the day time have ya?"

"Yeah well those are two things I wanted to tell you about but first sit down and have a look at these two sportsmen at the table."

Pillows went to the bar for three beers while Sockeye settled himself onto a stool with an unobtrusive view.

Five minutes ticked by while the three street savvy campaigners studied the boys' scams. Sockeye passed Pillows the look and lumbered to his feet.

"Hang on, hang on, hang on," from Nick "where are you two going?"

Sockeye turned back to Nick.

"You know damn well where I'm going, another hour of that shit will cost me ten grand a month in Yuppie money, they come here to pork fashion editors, not get rolled by off-duty P.L.F. (Palestinian Liberation Front).

"Aah, music to the ears. Ten a month you reckon? Look mate, you know these families stick like shit to a blanket, word gets back to Lakemba these boys have been flogged by some east Sydney ex -copper publican and in two days you will have bricks and petrol bombs raining through the windows.

What you need is some pissed off local citizen to talk to them."

Sockeye stopped and considered Nick's comment.

"Yeah, you could be right old son, but what might this concerned citizen cost a struggling small businessman?"

Nick chuckled.

"Struggling small businessman my arse! We both Know Tony O gave you this place, that's something else I want to talk about, but just for now, you know the rates. A gorilla each, ten percent, or mate's rates."

Nick's first price of a gorilla each, a thousand dollars per victim in underworld slang, while immediately rejected, told the publican he meant business. He knew Nick had picked up the "Ten grand a month" slip of the tongue so ten percent would cost him half of that, but like any good insurance man it was the third quote that caught his ear.

"And just what might these mate's rates be, me old mate?"

"Special price for you old son, a monkey up front, they'll be gone and won't want to come back".

"C'mon Nick, five hundred's a bit rich."

"The longer you haggle the less safe that ten a month is looking, by the way don't forget that price is up front, like me dear old dad told me.

"Never trust a copper".

Sockeye grumbled, reached into his pocket and pulled out a roll. He peeled off four hundreds and two fifties and handed them to Nick.

"Sure you'll be right on your own, old timer? I'll expect a discount if you need a hand."

"You just stay where you are copper, get your score cards ready and I'll show you some artistic content."

Nick left his seat and strolled across to the boys racking balls for their next game.

"Hey goat fuckers, tell your sister to come back next Friday night, the cricket team reckoned she's the best five bucks they ever spent."

At just over five and a half feet tall and a shade under seventy kilos Nick didn't look much.

Their response was just exactly what he expected.

The Mouth stood stunned, eyes bulged, jaw gaped. Muscles was quicker, he reversed the cue he was holding and swung the butt end at Nick's face.

Wrist and fingers loose, Nick flicked the second knuckle of his left forefinger into Mouth's right eye, caught the cue six inches from his face and drove a hard front kick into Muscles' bladder. He followed with a straight left, right upper cut, left hook. As Muscles' two schooners of orange juice emptied into his track suit pants, his knees gave way. Nick grabbed him by the hair and drove his broken jaw onto the table, blood and broken teeth sprayed across the green felt.

Confused and half blinded, Mouth lurched towards the noise. Nick slid a foot between his legs, dropped into a wide squat and drove a clenched fist up into his pelvis. Mouth's manhood was in the way. He screamed and draped forward across Nick's shoulders. Nick straightened his knees and surged upwards, maximum height, maximum speed and combined body weight he speared the young thief's right collar bone into the table's edge.

"Good noise," he thought as the bone shattered, the pain so great it turned Mouth's lights straight out.

After removing the loot from their pockets, he strolled back to his friends.

The bar patrons, for a moment struck dumb, burst into applause, Mouth and his mate hadn't endeared themselves to anyone.

When the battered thief came to, Nick returned and counselled him, and while they dragged their shattered bits into the street he considered what he next had to say to Sockeye.

The Plan

AS NICK SLID ONTO his stool Pillows glanced across to Sockeye and stated ''You should be taking a hundred back off him for cleaning, you know how hard it is to get blood out of that felt."

Sockeye agreed.

"He's right too, you old bastard, making a mess of me furniture."

"Leave it there mate, and put those teeth in a frame behind the bar. Add some of that `gangster chic` to the place. You can have that for free, something to remember me by".

Sockeye chuckled.

''Oh yeah, going to save me some money and bar yourself are ya?"

Nick sighed.

"More than that mate, as of today I'm out of the game; had enough mate. I'm leaving."

Pillows laughed outright.

''Yeah right, and do what? You love it you old thug, you won't stop until someone puts a bullet in your head."

"Funny you should say that mate. Same thought occurred to me about a month ago, just after that problem down Bondi way. Sat `round the house for a coupla weeks before I realised the only thing that really pisses me off is people. Phone won`t stop ringing, the more you do the more they want you to do, too many wet nights in cold dark alleys. Never any time for myself and like you say, one night they'll find me face down fulla holes."

Nick was a mate, a real one, and as this rambling whinge began to penetrate, the two old coppers shared a look of genuine concern.

"Shit Nick, that don't sound like you son."

"No mate, doesn't, does it. Started to scare myself actually. So I took a little trip. Got a plane up to Cairns, hired a car and drove up toward Port Douglas. Saw it on one of those holiday shows. Anyway, middle of town, Macrossan Street, there's this indoor /outdoor place called the Ironbar. Thought, yeah, that's me, so I stopped in for a beer and a steak.

Best thing I ever did. Met this Kiwi barmaid who took me there. One of the boys on the door's an old student of mine, ran away to the deep north 'bout five years ago. Tells me this bird works twelve hours a day every day three months a year. Anyway we got to talking and she's told me the story. Got this thirty-eight-foot catamaran, works enough to pay for spares, supplies and anti-foul and spends most of her year floating around the reef and the coast.

Got on pretty well really. Anyway, got Dobson, that's the doorman, to have a chat with the boss, worked out what two weeks off work would cost her and talked her into a little private charter. She took me up north of the Daintree River, 'bout sixty clicks north of Port and parked off a place called Cow Bay. Para-fucking-dise mate. No people, no pollution, coral trout and crayfish jump out of the water into the pan, mangoes everywhere, 'stead of eight dollars each up Bellevue Hill, and a nice little pub 'bout two miles inland. That's me mate."

"I figure for a hundred grand I can set up for the rest of my life. And a real life too, instead of this bloody Tarantino movie I been living. No one shooting at ya. No bastard trying to stick knives or broken bottles in ya. Five acres, a kit house, couple of solar panels and sling a hammock between two palm trees."

Sockeye took a moment then remarked, "Bullshit Nick, you just done your nuts over another Wahine, don't know what it is with you and these bloody Kiwis, and anyway, where are you gunna get a hundred big ones?"

Nick's eyes narrowed, Sockeye slowly eased out of arm's reach.

"I'm serious Ray, you might be right about the Wahine but I'll be a lot better off finding out about her up there than sitting here looking at your rough head. As for the hundred, I've got a meeting with Tony O tomorrow to call in my marker. That's what I wanted to ask you. How do you think he'll handle a hundred? It's a big ask."

Pillows broke the growing tension.

"Come on mate, have a think, everything Tony's got he owes to you, he fronted five times that to put us in here, and all we ever did was keep our mouths shut. Thirty years and you've never asked for anything, he'll give you the hundred and beg you to take more. He might be the biggest crook in town but he pays his debts."

Sockeye chimed in.

"Too true mate, if that's what you really want all you have to do is ask and he'll give it to ya. One thing though, what are you going to do about Dave?"

The question caught Nick out.

"What do you mean, 'do about Dave'?   He's doing fine, got a good steady job doing the books for that club of Brian's up Springfield Avenue."

"Sockeye and Pillows both dropped their eyes before the publican slowly added.

"Look mate, I know you like to play your cards close to your chest but anybody with his eyes open knows he's been your apprentice since you did your thing after his big night. He's good yeah, but he's young and he's moving in a hard world. One day he'll be good enough but just now he don't have your contacts and he don't have your nouse."

Nick squirmed, anxious the affection he held for his recent protege shouldn't show. It was a conditioned reflex, hard years had taught him any weakness displayed would quickly be seized by an enemy and turned against him or those he cared for. Now in the company of friends, he shook off his misgivings.

Pillows jibed in.

"He's been in here twice in the last couple of weeks looking for you. Don't know why but some people seem to miss your ugly old head when you go missing. You told him yet?"

Nick relaxed and replied evenly.

"He'll be right, he's invited me to dinner tonight to meet some new girlfriend. I'll find the right moment to tell him. Don't worry, whatever happens I don't leave anyone out on a limb."

It was lightly said, but Nick was a man of his word, and he didn't realise just what those words were to cost him.

CHRISTA

SOCKEYE DROPPED THE INCREASINGLY serious conversation and switched to a lighter note.

"So son, your last day in town, eh? Gunna spend it sitting here drinking me hard earned money?"

Nick cleared his throat.

"No mate, just stopped by to say goodbye and get a feel on how to approach Tony tomorrow. Got a couple more stops to make."

With that he shook hands twice, stepped out the door and down the two marble treads into Elizabeth Street.

He looked out over the fall of the hill, over White City, the home of the city's tennis elite, the private school football grounds, home of the city's future political and economic rulers, and the beautiful Sydney Harbour's Rushcutters Bay, home of the city's Royal Sailing Yacht Squadron.

He wondered again at the strange twist of town non-planning that jammed these bastions of privilege hard up against the arse end of King's Cross, home of some of the city's most greedy, violent and amoral characters.

"Not that different I suppose, same wolves different sheepskins, she's a hard old town, I'm not going to miss her much."

Nick strolled down the steepening street, turned left opposite the newly opened art gallery in Hargrave Street and continued to gently walk off his few beers with the boys. His destination, Bayswater Towers, was still out of view but his "back of my hand" familiarity with the town's geography plus a similar familiarity with one of the security complex's residents turned his head towards the multi-storey apartment block. He turned right at the aptly named Cascade Street and let gravity power his progress to Glenmore Road. He laughed quietly at himself.

"Good thing it's all downhill, Christa seems to be taking a bit more out of me every time I see her nowadays. Good time to be saying goodbye, best to go out with a bang."

As Nick neared the bottom of the hill, the four way intersection shrouded him in a fog of teenage memories. The taxi base, hard on his left where long-lost brother Terry spent half his working life, Trumper Park to his right, scene of joyful victories and crushing defeats while Nick sweated out two years' banishment from his beloved Rugby League, playing the then, for Sydney, upstart game of A.F.L.

Further on the left the old Dunlop rubber factory, across whose sawtooth, asbestos- sheeted roofs local boys would pursue those out of ground balls kicked by over-zealous full forwards.

Another hard lesson learnt the day Paulie crashed through the asbestos sheeting to find thirty feet of air and an untimely death on the concrete factory floor.

Nick watched, learning quickly, as Paulie's two mates traded profanity and punches for possession of the ball

Paulie cast aside as he fell to his death. No room for sentiment on these streets.

As Nick passed the dip in the road he sloughed off the caustic memory.

"Come on you silly old fart, you'll want to show a lot more sparkle than this when you hit the Dutch girl's door, bottle of Moet should do the trick."

A quick stop at Bayswater Cellars for a bottle of vintage sparkle, then across the traffic- choked artery to the apartment block's intercom panel to signal his arrival.

Christa checked the video security system and recognised Nick's head.

A thirty-year-old flamboyant redhead, mistress to what the tabloids labelled `a prominent racing identity,` Christa had met Nick five years previously when her bookmaker boyfriend suffered a temporary cash flow problem. He figured two weeks at the Perth casino, where a nod and a wink to a friendly croupier removed most of the chance in the game, should be enough. Nick was hired and took up residence in her second bedroom in case either of the owners of his principle debts decided to express their anger in his absence. Two temporary employees of a cranky gambler showed up with a good enough story for the neighbours to let them past the security system and orders to "do something ugly" to the missing bookie's favourite trophy.

By the time the leader of the pair was released from his oxygen tent and entered a general ward, Christa had overcome her surprise and expressed her appreciation.

By the time he was walking, their strawberries and cream coated sexual romp had calmed to a deep mutual respect.

The thirty-year-old girl held no illusions about her career, she knew she was her own best asset and literally trained her arse off to maintain her facade. On arrival Nick had

prowled the apartment. The stay-cycle, weights machine, heavy bag and floor to ceiling ball filling the third bedroom surprised him. Her daily hour and a half use of the room plus the extra half hour on a yoga mat before the floor-to-ceiling windows left him impressed.

With poise, intelligence and European elegance she graced the boardrooms and mansions she visited with Bruce the bookie. She made him look a class act and was rewarded accordingly. The flaming red hair, six pack abs and twenty thousand dollar Hollywood clinic implants didn't hurt a lot either.

She pressed the buttons which allowed access to the lift lobby and activated the elevator controls, Nick rode to the eleventh floor humming. He knocked and entered the apartment.

Christa greeted him in an deep blue silk kimono, her hair a single thick braid down the centre of her back, she kissed him briefly, took the bottle from his hands.

"Moet vintage, you trying to charm me Nick?"

She crossed to an ice bucket set on a wide glass table overlooking the bay then turned and smiled at Nick as he followed, then let the rippling silk slide from her shoulders as she flowed back towards him. But for a pair of brief silk pants she was naked beneath the kimono and as they came together she nuzzled into his neck and eased his shirt over his head.

Circling a nipple with her tongue she was rewarded with a deep and prolonged sigh, then switched to the other nipple, gently nibbling, she could feel Nick's body quiver as she sunk to her knees and loosened his belt with her teeth.

"Whoa girl, whoa, whoa, got something I gotta tell ya."

She reached down and undid his shoelaces, Nick lifted her to her feet.

"I know you've got something to say Nick, I don't want to hear it. Sockeye rang just after you left the Windsor, he figured you'd stop here next so he rang to warn me. I've got a spa full of bubbles and a head full of ideas to help you change your mind."

"Changing my mind is not going to happen girl. But let's not let those bubbles go to waste, how 'bout I bring that ice bucket, you bring some glasses and you show me that spa."

With that Nick stepped out of his shoes and the pool of his trousers, picked up the ice bucket and headed for the spa.

Christa busied herself in the breakfast nook and followed him with two glasses and a pair of shortened drinking straws, their ends plugged by her right thumb.

Nick was up to his chest in foam when she entered the lightly steamed room and knelt by his head, she placed one straw in her nose, leant forward, offered the other to her playmate and released her thumb as they both snorted deeply.

She slid into the tub and onto his lap, they embraced tightly and said "Aaah" for about

three minutes as the pure Peruvian flake cocaine bounced from their brains to their genitals and back.

As Christa's flash began to taper she asked coyly.

"After this can I show you my bedroom?"

Nick replied.

"After that you can show me your bedroom, your gym, your couch and the top of your fridge if you like. Just don't kill me girl!"

They laughed and lunged at each other as water exploded across the room.

Two hours later Nick slowly untangled himself from the satin sheets and eased to his

feet. Christa opened an eye and slapped his butt. "Where you going, you horny old bastard?"

Nick jumped and replied.

"The shower first, then North Queensland; weren't you listening you dippy bimbo or are those cute little ears painted on?"

"You know it won't happen Nick, and what are you going to do about Dave?"

He continued to the ensuite and called over his shoulder as he turned on the stinging spray.

"That's the second time today someone's said that. What do you mean do

about Dave?"

The happily bruised redhead followed him into the cubicle. "Did you know he got that nickname from Brian's wife for the childish way he treats his women, or should I say little girls. Without you to cover his arse, in three months every woman in town is going to know he's frightened of 'em. They'll start to hate him for the way he compensates, and you know how popular you get with the boys when all the real women in town can't stand you."

While talking, she'd reached around and taken Nick in a soapy two-handed grip. He

arched his back into her breasts and said.

"Don't worry about Dave girl I'll have a little talk with him before I leave." Then turned, lifted her thighs around his waist and thanked her for the hospitality.

DINNER

PEE WEE PUSHED HIS chair back and stood to answer the phone. At six and a half foot tall and as wide as a Darlinghurst doorway it was an event worth watching.

"He's smoothing out," thought Nick "very little effort, easy shift of balance and a glide to the balls of his feet. Not the old habit of grinding his heels into the ground and lurching his shoulders skywards. Maybe it is time to stop calling him Pee Wee. Maybe she's right, it's time for him to stop behaving like a kid. Good thing it's a quiet night, I'll pull him aside later and we'll have a chat."

Nick hadn't yet broken his news to Dave. Considering Christa's comments from that afternoon and having Dave's newest mindless conquest introduced as he arrived, he figured a few well-chosen words concerning the young giant's choice of and behaviour towards the fairer sex a good idea, before telling him his travel plans. He had mentioned there was something he wanted to talk about when they had a free ten minutes.

Kate resumed her monologue on white limos, catholic cathedrals and $5,000 bridal gowns, dragging Nick's reluctant attention back to the dinner table.

"Christ, another private school princess. Where'd he find this airhead?" thought Nick.

"And when do you and Dave plan this happy event Katie?"

A perplexed shadow flicked through the bright, young, empty eyes as she replied,

"Dave? Who's Dave?"

"Why, your inamorata of course, princess. Surely if you're about to embark upon one of the great loves of the twentieth century you should at least know your crewmate's name."

"Oh he'll always be Pee Wee to me. I'm going to dress him in sky blue bicycle shorts and yellow singlet and parade him at Tamarama Beach. The girls from Kincoppal will just drool."

"Parade him? You make him sound like a cross between a Ken doll and your uncle's stud bull."

"How did you know Uncle Sidney had bulls?"

"You all have uncles with a stud somewhere, princess. That's why you and your friends don't have to have real jobs."

"I've heard of you Nick Fallon, and when Pee Wee said he was inviting you I was prepared to give you the benefit of the doubt, but when I tell him what you just said you'll never enter this house again!"

"Excuse me folks," Pee Wee from the door. "I hate to do this Kate, but there seems to be an irregularity at the club and Brian has asked me to drop by."

"Well, he can just wait until you've finished dinner and seen your guests home. You really must learn to be more forceful Pee."

"I'm sorry sweet but duty calls. Must earn those fun tickets if we're going to have any fun."

Nick stirred.

"Mind if I tag along Dave? Kate and I seem to have come to know each other well enough for the moment and a little air would be pleasant."

A safe half-block from the gate Dave's grin burst through his clenched cheeks, "Jesus Nick. Your inamorata princess! Where does a detoxed old hippie like you dig up a poncy- arsed turn of phrase like that?"

"Heard that did you? Sorry mate but I can't help myself. Every time I meet one of these granddaughters of the squattocracy you drag home from Oxford Street, I get struck by my celtic racial memory."

"Get up on that triangle you 'oribble little Irishman. Whack, whack, whack. Right now, on with these leg irons, down into that hold and off to Van Dieman's Land with you, you nasty bloody Catholic you. Spend the rest of your life pushing cart loads of pommies up and down Parramatta Road."

"Come on Nick, that's a bit harsh."

"Harsh mate? Harsh? Have you seen the used cart yards out there now. It's become enshrined in Australian folk tradition son. Every weekend shoddy carts full of middle class pommie immigrants cruising Parramatta Road looking for a sturdy brace of Irishmen to yoke to the front bumper of the Cortina. It never ends mate, it never ends."

"You're strange Nick."

"Unique my old son, unique."

"Face it Nick, you're as diplomatic as mace in the face. I don't know how you've lasted so long in the game. I only invited you tonight 'cause sweet Kate has already made her donation to dear old Dave's jewellery box and it's time for her to be moving along."

"Oh yeah, and how are you going to tell little sweetheart that I'm in and she's out?"

"She knows I'm an honourable man Nick. When I explain how I can't let my poor old karate teacher, who's taken one too many kicks to the head, stumble off friendless into aged infirmity she'll see why I have to let my one true chance at love pass as a ship in the night."

"That's a fair line of blarney you've grown yourself. Tricky that, in a jew."

"I'm a tricky jew, Nick."

"Tricky enough to get her to add to that Rolex repository the Commonwealth Bank holds for you down town?"

"Let you in on a little secret Nick, there's three boxes now and if you keep helping with the turnover you're in for ten percent."

"Ten percent?"

"Yeah mate, ten percent."

"Done son! Now, what's Brian's problem?"

Brian's Problem

NICK DROVE INTO THE alley and parked next to the club truck. An '83 Ford panelvan with imposing custom-built bull bar and vertically opening rear doors. It could quite handily transport fruit and veges from the markets, crates of alcohol from various low cost sales or in a pinch, up to ten of the off-duty street doormen who habitually drank in Brian's club. Like most drinkers, for a pat on the back and a dozen Jack Daniels, they'd usually be happy to do the publican small favours.

As Nick stepped from the car he took a good look at the security standing two steps up under the light by the back door. Just over six foot tall, twenty three maybe twenty four years old, blue eyes like ice picks, blonde bristle cut hair, painted on t-shirt and solid muscle down to his toenails.

Nick spoke quietly across the roof of the car to Dave.

"This the new guy eh. He looks the goods. Has he got any brains. What's his name?"

Dave replied in a soft voice.

"Name's Kevin. As for smarts, you never believe anyone anyway, find out for yourself."

Nick locked the car, took a few steps down the alley and threw his keys to the new guy.

From his size and position of club paymaster, Kevin had recognised Dave immediately, Nick he hadn't met, but he had been told. He caught the keys and his week changed. One month out of South Auckland and already working the back door of the most talked about club in King's Cross, Kev felt he was finally getting where he wanted to be. If only he could think of something clever to say to the constant gaggle of half a dozen strippers looking straight through him, trying to attract the attention of someone inside.

You paid twenty dollars to walk in Brian's front door, the back door was strictly invitation only.

As he entered the circle of light Nick asked, "Mind if we go on through Kev, and ah, would you mind keeping an eye on my car?"

"This time Nick, but don't make a habit of it," he replied with a grin.

Two short sentences told Nick and Kevin what they needed to know about each other. With handshakes, knowing looks and real smile Kev ushered them through the door. Those two short sentences also had another effect, as six sets of scheming female eyes struck various parts of the testosterone-pumped doorman's anatomy with one common thought.

"Wonder what I can do to this guy to get inside?"

Nick knew it and Kevin knew he knew it. He'd been thinking about what to do if any of the local junkies tried to steal one of the club vehicles and decided if anyone looked like leaning on his new mate Nick's ride, he just might have to rip their arms and legs off as well.

Through the door and into the members' bar. A muted room, where by either common consent or a strange quirk of acoustics, conversations seemed not to carry from one table to another. Comfortable though. Patrons could feel free to indulge in whatever party favourites were flavour of the month, enjoy those friendly gestures men and women feel inclined to share from time to time or with a friendly gesture, summon a trusted fellow businessman to discuss the day's profits and liabilities.

They split at the door, threading parallel paths through the tables and booths, acknowledging greetings stated and signalled. Each shared the same thought, "Same thing everywhere, make the customer feel like the owner and he's yours for generations".

They met at Phil's stool. Phil controlled the door to the punter's bar and kept tabs on most parts of the club.

"Brian says grab a drink, he'll be through in a minute."

Nick and Dave breasted the bar. Unlike the broad range of liquors on display in the public areas, the labels on these bottles actually described what was likely to be found inside.

"Cointreau and ice and a glass of orange juice."

Cheryl stepped from the far side of the bar, grabbed Nick by the ears and kissed him square on the lips.

"That's for last month, I won't forget."

Dave coughed half his orange juice across the bar and swung his startled eyes to Nick.

"You porking the ice queen?"

"Nuh, nothing of the sort son. Just a little gratitude for the first aid."

Cheryl was regarded as the most dependable of the club's female staff, so when Nick overheard Phil complain to Brian she hadn't rung in to explain her absence from her Saturday night shift he decided to pay her a visit.

The Surry Hills studio she shared with her rumoured to be artistic boyfriend had a simple lock so Nick let himself in to find Cheryl naked, gagged and handcuffed to a steam pipe, a painful stretch above her head.

Boyfriend sat a metre from her, his back to the door.

"There's a mistake," thought Nick.

A straightened wire coat hanger across his bare thighs and a syringe full of cocaine being pressed into the crook of his left elbow. Eyes shut tight as the drug rolled through his brain, starburst still shots of painful possibilities lived short and lurid lives on the inside of his eyelids.

Not wishing to interrupt a couple at play, Nick slipped silently to Cheryl's side to whisper an enquiry in her ear and unclip the leather gag sufficiently to discover she had definitely not volunteered for the night's S&M fantasy.

After a short conversation, boyfriend agreed to mind Cheryl's place while Nick iced her blistered wrists, murmured those words that seemed most appropriate and tucked her in bed with a near perfect blend of Dr. Fallon's Valium, Panadol and Scotch cure all.

The coat hanger caught his eye. An ever-curious bugger, he tried an experiment or two. A musical, whistling kind of noise, quite pleasant really. No sound from the test dummy's double-taped mouth of course, no need to disturb the neighbours, but the distance the eye balls bulged suggested quite a sting.

From time to time some people proved a trifle reticent in conversation, and while a cockroach-filled plastic bag applied as headpiece for a minute or two usually elicited enthusiasm, even in Bondi collecting all those cockys could be a time consuming pain in the arse. More durable than a car aerial, an often available hanger may well be worth remembering. Then he and boyfriend went for a walk in the night.

Raiding the refrigerator for ice, he noticed a phone on its hook on the kitchen wall. "Don't suppose she'd mind the price of a call if I cleared her arse with Brian."

He didn't like lying to his friend but knew some things were best kept secret. "Bloody little idiot has scalded both her wrists and was too sore and embarrassed to ring in. I'll put some ice packs on 'em and put her to bed. She should be right by tomorrow night."

Cheryl woke to find Nick changing cool cloths over her wrists. He told her that her boyfriend would not be back.

She believed him.

She was grateful.

Nick looked forward to discovering just how grateful. The clues so far looked promising.

Brian slid through the door, crossed eyes with the unlikely pair, tapped his head in the military "to me" gesture and strode to an already heavily occupied booth. Tom and Jerry heavily occupied the booth. One black German and one white maori, they filled the four person booth.

Dave was first to ask. "What's up?"

Brian began to explain.

The soccer finals had created a bad result. One of the city's inner west ethnic ghettoes had defeated the neighbouring enclave's team. In the true spirit of sportsmanship and demonstrating their hearty acceptance of Australia's multiculturalism, both teams decided to hold a riot. Everybody came. Once the State Police, with their riot control, Tactical Response Group and bitey dogs arrived, the winning team's captain figured it would be safer to load up the club bus with as many players and supporters as wanted to party on, and head into the Cross to bash and fuck as many working girls as possible.

"They're only sluts, who's going to care?" asked the hero.

Brian cared.

Nick cared.

Tom and Jerry cared.

A lot of guys cared.

Brian was rounding up a dozen. With the right guys he felt a dozen would be enough to properly express his feelings. Notwithstanding the fact that two of the working houses paid him handsomely to do just that.

He began to explain.

"We've got a team of dago soccer players just steamrolled into Peaches and Cream, kicked old Eric into dog shit, ripped the phones out and spent an hour rooting the girls and smashing the place up. Blues is watching them and they're headed towards Heather's."

Heather's Feathers that is.

One of the principal brothels of Potts Point's back streets, Heather had become financially wealthy during her first decade of working, her real power devolved through the next two decades of collecting closet skeletons both within and without the milieu.

A good friend.

A dangerous enemy.

Brian's patron.

"With you four we've got six, I need six more guys right now!"

Nick corkscrewed up to perch on the arm of the booth, temporarily at eye level with his friend.

"Jesus, look at this," he thought, "I'm living in the land of the fucking giants, I got to meet some human sized people," then voiced his question.

"Hang on Brian, there's enough muscle in this room to turn those guys into a stain. What aren't you saying?"

Brian shrugged.

"Tony O, seems one of these arseholes is his grandson. I need `Unknowns`."

"What for? Tony's probably sitting down at The Maze right now watching all this through his runners. How's he not going to know your team belted his ward?"

Brian smiled with a cynical grin.

"You in my team now Nick?"

"You and Tony both know how I'm going to behave in this, and no I'm not in anyone's team Brian. I'm talking about Tom and Jerry and you and Blues. There could be a war in this. Get Heather to keep them busy for an hour. I'll round up some of the friends and you guys won't have to go near the place."

Brian went quiet for a moment, sipped his drink and looked quizzically at Nick's eyes. Strangely, they weren't haggard or anything like road maps. Thoughtfully, he started.

"You haven't been paying attention have you? Tony's getting greedy again. He knows where these kids are and he knows what they're doing. He hasn't sent anyone to tell them to stop. The war's already on Nick, I'm just trying to keep it between Tony and me. Don't want the young blokes shooting each other over breakfast at Adam's.

Tom and Jerry spend most of their wages with the girls so it's not possible to keep them out of it, Blues goes where I go and, as for me, this is real personal. He wants my business. If I can shame him into standing up himself, I'll beat the living shit out of him and even his old man won't say boo. Mate, even the heavies working for him don't like him. All I have to do is give this team a personal slap, with some mystery back up, and Tony will go quiet for a while. If he doesn't stand up, he can still gracefully apologise for his grandson's behaviour, keep to his own business and nobody loses. He just gets to know there's more to old Briany boots than meets the eye."

"You know it's got to happen between you and him one day."

"Yeah, but like you say Nick, my time and my place, not his. By the way Nick, what is it with you and Tony? I've seen you slap his boys in public and he does nothing."

"I only ever slap them for bad manners Brian, not for business. Young Tony may be a pig but his father was, and still is, a gentleman. We, aaah, we were friends a long time ago."

"Old Tony is very old Nick."

"I know Brian, I know. I also know six people that not many other people know. See you at Heather's in one hour."

"Hang on Nick, just one small detail."

Brian stepped across the booth and draped a beefy arm over the smaller man's shoulders.

"What's all this going to cost an old mate, old mate."

"You know how it is Brian, nothing in life is free, ten percent, old mate."

Brian looked pained, Dave looked mystified. He had to ask.

"Ten percent of what Nick?"

"Whatever the club makes tonight Dave. Seeing I've been away a couple of weeks, I could use a little earn."

As the club's new official bookkeeper, Dave was not too happy.

"That's not a little earn, Nick."

"I'm going to have to pay all the boys. You know what payrolls are like Dave."

Nick grinned slid from the booth arm and started for the door.

"Come on mister bookkeeper let's go find some mister nobodies."

As Dave and Nick stepped into the lane, Kevin extricated himself from a tangle of stroking hands and whispered lies to hand Nick the club truck keys.

He winked and spoke quietly, "Don't go getting greedy there Kev," threw the keys to Dave and said more loudly, "You drive long legs. I'll find Fuji, at least one of them will be carrying a blade. Let's have that swisho phone of yours for a bit."

Dave drew the half house brick-sized mobile phone from a harness over his left ribs and mocked his friend.

"Just too cheap to buy your own, you penny-pinching catholic."

"When they get down to Dick Tracey watches they got me son. Even you gotta carry that thing in a sling, I'd need a backpack."

"By the way Nick, Phil told me one of these arseholes dropped old Eric the cleaner with a kick. Seems he's some kind of black belt deadly killer."

"Kicked old Eric did he? Well, we'll just have to be on the lookout for him, won't we? Take us along Victoria Street and up past John's place, maybe we can get a look at them before they get to Heather's."

"I'll drive past but I'm not stopping. Even if we pick Blues up, that's still too many for three of us."

"Don't worry mate, no playing heroes tonight, I'm not about to give these fuckers any chances at all. I just want to see whether it would be better to use thinkers or the Brute Squad."

"Why not just bring everybody?"

"Wages son. Like I told Brian, I'm going to have to pay the guys, asking them to risk a knife in the ribs for nothing would be a bit rude."

Dave still wasn't satisfied.

"Ten percent of tonight's take would pay for a fair sized team Nick."

"Not going all sookie on me are you, since you've gone back to accountancy? Don't worry mate, like I said, I don't intend giving these arseholes any kind of chance at all. Just like to have something left in the kitty when it's all over. Got something coming up where a coupla extra bucks'll be handy."

"Oh yeah, and what's that?"

"One thing at a time son, don't worry I'll tell you 'bout it a bit later. Now let's get going while they're still on the street."

Nick dialled, Dave drove.

Fuji and The Cops

WHILE THE RIGHT-HAND BALISONG knife snapped open and shut, whirring in imitation of a butterfly's flight, the dancer's left hand guided its own surgical steel blade across the taut skin of his left calf, removing most of the theatrical oil.

An accustomed thunder on the dressing room door announced the backstage manager's desire to converse with the show's star act.

"Hey shithead! Phone call, be quick with it."

Out the dressing room door, down the narrow corridor and into the showbill-papered nook that George grandly nominated his office.

"Yeah?"

"Fuji?"

"Nick? What's up?"

"Got a team of twenty or so soccer players making a mess. Got Brian and young Tony politics, got Peaches and old Eric trashed and smashed. They're headed for Heather's and I'm expecting knives. You interested?"

"I'm a dancer Nick!"

"You're a cab driver Fuji. Two days a week on stage don't make you John Travolta."

I'm a dancer Nick!"

"That why Uncle Jesus bundled you up and smuggled you out of Manila in the middle of the night?"

"They weren't supposed to die Nick."

"And I'm not supposed to be old and poor, you're not supposed to be a cab driver and Peaches ain't supposed to be closed tonight. Heather ain't supposed to have the name, phone number, fax number and address of every sexually twisted, cocaine addicted, major producer, director and show biz financer in her I.O.U. book. If you really are a dancer, doing Heather a favour would be the best audition you could do in this town."

"Where, when?"

"Brian's place,soon as you can,we'll put the team together there then hit 'em at Heather's"

"I'm in Enmore, Nick."

"Take a cab Fooj."

"Ha ha very funny, see you Nick."

"Half hour Fooj."

Nick hung up the phone and turned his attention to the trail of bleeding drunks, shattered car windows and upturned garbage cans which pointed to the party group further down the late night street.

Dave spied a flying trash can as it arced out into the street and bounced off the roof of a passing Honda. He turned to his friend and mentor.

"They're moving mighty slow and making a lot of noise Nick, at this rate the uniforms will get them before we're all lined up."

"Not a chance mate. Bet you two spot they show up ten minutes after the ambulance."

"Two hundred? No way, you only bet when you've paid the jockey."

"Not a fix son, where coppers are concerned I'm omniscient. Matter of fact, if I close my eyes I can see MacCauley and Thompson right now."

"Bullshit, go on."

Nick smiled, closed his eyes, nestled back into his seat and murmured something like

"Oom mani patri soom, Oom mani patri soom."

"And what do you see O Wrinkled One?" from Dave.

"I see two men, one in an expensive crumpled suit, one in blue pants with a pullover hiding the silver crowns on his shoulders. They're sitting in Brian's office, pouring Jack Daniels down their throats like it was free, and whingeing about shitty working conditions and skinny pay packets."

"You can hear them too?"

"Mate, I'm so in touch I can hear what the girls are thinking."

"What girls?"

"The ones kneeling in front of the cops dopey! They can get a drink anywhere on the strip, that quality Brazilian marching powder keeps them on their knees."

"Sorry, sorry, I got caught up in the mystic mystery of the moment, speak on O Wizened One."

"Hang on another vision is coming through, the blonde is starting to cramp in her left leg, the redhead's happy she picked Thompson and his pencil dick and they're both wishing Brian would lay out another line to pay for their heads going up and down and get that shitty taste of pork out of their mouths."

"You sure that's omniscience and not just something that happens every Sunday
night?"

"Come no Dave, you know drugs, alcohol and blows to the head have killed my short-term memory. You don't really believe I can remember back week to week, do you. That's why I've had to develop these extra senses."

"Well either way, omniscience or public service pay day, no bet!"

Nick groaned. "That's the problem with you young blokes, every time I show you something it costs me money."

Blues stepped out in front of the car.

Bill the Girl

DAVE BRAKED TO A halt.

Blues stepped to the passenger side of the car, removed his hat and stuck his sun-glassed head through the passenger window.

"G'day Nick, Pee Wee." He turned his head and peered into the back of the panelvan, and pulled his sunglasses half way down his nose to be sure there was no one there.

"You guys here for the boys down the street?"

"Yes mate," from Dave.

"They're drunk but they're young, fit and mean. Four of us aren't enough."

Dave missed it and replied. "Brian's got Tom and Jerry on tap up at the club, Fuji's on his way and Nick reckons he can pull out enough guys to make up an even dozen. Don't worry, there'll be enough of us to go 'round by the time they step out of Heather's."

Nick interrupted.

"What do you mean four, Blues?"

"Bill went past about two minutes ago on that bike of hers. She slowed down, had a look at them and turned up Challis Avenue. She's with us isn't she?"

"Yeah. She would be with us, but nobody's told her we're with her yet. She'll set an ambush up on Macleay Street, probably puncture a few of 'em and then get that tight little arse of hers bashed and fucked. Jump in Blues, we'll head her off."

Six feet of silken skin, a cascade of blonde hair with the heart of a lion. Prussian-bred Wilhelmina Famler starred as East Sydney's very own Valkyrie. Her once aristocratic father had washed up on the shores of Madagascar with the remnant of his war-torn family. The work was hard, but with three sturdy sons and faith in their future, the family strived and thrived.

In '58 son number one took his new M.G. to the top of a mountain by road and back to the valley by air. In '59 a proud Prussian son went drinking with the son of a Boer, and in an arrogant drunken mistake, proved the long-held theory that proud Prussian fists were no match for an old Vortrekker knife. By '61, with son number three coughing his lungs into a foul-smelling bowl, an angry old man told his ever obedient wife he needed another boy.

Perhaps as the karmic repayment to an aged unrepentant Nazi, perhaps a cosmic reply to his own arrogance, perhaps the spirits of Madagascar simply decided they'd had enough of troublesome Famler men.

As the ever faithful wife Wilhelmina slipped out of the world, her baby daughter fought her way in. She left behind her a strong and beautiful girl child and an angry old man with a crushed black heart and a bitter soul. He survived long enough to feed his daughter Willy many meals, pain, spartan discipline, confused sexuality and the foundations of a ferocious anger, before burying his last son, putting a bullet in his brain, and unleashing her upon an unsuspecting world.

She'd entered Sydney as a whispered rumour, some unusually pretty street worker was rolling sailors on their way back to their Woolloomooloo Bay berths from the working houses in Rushcutters Bay's back streets.

Rumour was almost true.

The club owners took their profits in the crowded streets between these suburbs.

The houses didn't need the bad P.R.

Someone asked Brian to look.

She was seen.

She was surrounded.

She knocked Dave out.

Nick, and others, were impressed.

She was trussed and set before Heather.

Heather was furious. "What the fuck did you think you were doing? You're not even working, just a fucking thief!"

The casual off-the-cuff comment, delivered with a back hand slap, received a startling reply. A ten minute fury powered, tear-oiled tirade describing a fearful fantasy world of young girls with a three-month shelf life, chained to narrow cots satisfying the more disgusting desires of drunken seamen. Her actions not greed, but an unexplained quest for vengeance.

Heather stopped, open mouthed, thought for a moment and made a decision.

"Don't know if you've ever been in a brothel girl, but surely not one in this town, you should meet the girls."

Nick relaxed, he'd wanted this strange girl to walk out in one piece and now he knew she would.

Heather pulled the blonde avenger to her feet and ushered her into the girls' waiting room.

Disbelief, giggles and laughter. A dozen or more attractive, intelligent women attired in expensive lingerie and slit-legged designer gowns. Moet Chandon, fresh cappuccinos, the occasional skinny joint as a rarely required aphrodisiac or a half nose of Peruvian flake if the circumstance required. Stimulants and relaxants readily at hand but never so much use to harm the finely sculptured bodies and minds with which these career women compiled incomes to make a bank manager blush.

Bill was out of a job and Nick was happy to offer her another. Similar work, but with a hat not so black, just a shade of grey. Bill was happy to take it but still maintained a protective friendship with Heather and her staff.

She crouched now in an alley way, a knife in either hand with just the silver toe cap of her left boot dimly reflecting from a lazy street.

"There she is Dave. Pull up."

Dave braked in the middle of the street.

"Where?"

Nick pointed. "See, there, low in the corner of the lane. She bought those winkle pickers for kicking guys in the arse, keeps 'em sharp and shiny as."

Then louder. "Bill! Get over here."

The girl came cautiously out of the dark and approached the van.

"Nick is that you?"

He opened the door and stepped towards her.

"Of course I'm me you dill, who else would I be?"

She hurled herself into his chest and threw both arms around his neck.

"Jesus I thought you were dead. Where have you been?"

Blues and Dave exchanged looks of surprise.

He slipped her question and laughed.

"Oh yeah, trying to make sure are you? Put those bloody knives away before you cut my head off and I am dead."

Before Nick gave Bill any work, as with all players, he needed to see just what she had. They ran, they swam, tried bag work, light and heavy sparring then grappling. The final straw was submission holds. Like two minutes before a thunderstorm, the air grew electric. They'd both felt it and known it for what it was. Over coffee they made the only sensible decision. Armed with everything necessary to drink, snort, smoke and rub in, they booked into The Sebel Town House and took three days to flatten their sexual batteries. An exercise designed to cut tension and prevent future mistakes, it created a lingering affection and remained their secret.

"We got Fuji coming for blade work. How'd you get here?"

"Nadine. Soon as they left Peaches she went next door to the pub and called me."

"You're going to have to work on your image girl. She must think you're superwoman to take that many on your own, and you should know better."

''Get in, 'stead of sticking a couple of 'em, we'll get a few more troops together and ambush the lot of the bastards. I don't want any of them getting away."

She tried to disagree.

"Heather's is just around the corner Nick. By the time you get anyone together they'll have done the same as they did at Peaches. I'll stay here and slow 'em down."

"Get in stupid. I'm not going to spend you just to buy fifteen minutes. That's not long enough anyway, even if you were just a throwaway. Sit still for a moment and you might learn something."

Nick smiled sarcastically and added.

"You can trust me girl, I used to sell used cars."

He turned back to the van.

"Blues, we're leaving you here. Get 'round to Heather's and tell her to let them in.

Tell her to make 'em think old Tony owns the place or he's a silent partner or something, that should keep 'em polite for a bit. I'll ring her when we're lined up and she can show 'em out. And tell her to be sure to close that street door behind 'em. Don't want to give 'em anywhere to run."

Heather's and its customers valued their privacy. To ensure this, the lady of the house had had a three-metre block wall built to enclose the front of the place.

With a solid timber gate set in the centre, a surveillance camera mounted in the rain shelter arch and an intercom panel mounted on the adjacent block work, security was also improved. Nick figured if he could catch them still milling out the front telling each other macho lies, a dozen good guys could flank them and pin them against the wall like sheep.

Bill opened the back doors and got in, Blues stepped out and walked around to Nick's window.

"Where are you going? How long are you going to be?"

Nick stuck his head out and replied. "We're going to duck over to Redfern for a bit, should be back in about half an hour. Find a spot out of sight opposite Heather's and if Fuji shows up, tell him to wait. We won't be long. I'll ring Brian and let him know what's going on."

Blues nodded, "Okay Nick, see you there."

They shared a handshake then Blues headed off to set the trap.

Nick turned to Dave.

"Okay son let's boot it.Redfern."

Dave turned left on Macleay Street and down past Garden Island, the Navy base that supplied horny sailors to the girls and emptied military pay packets into the tills of the clubs on the strip. Past the face of the Woolloomooloo docks and left again on Forbes Street they headed to the South side of town.

Bill asked Nick where he'd disappeared to, and while he gave her an abbreviated story of his tropical travels, he kept an eye on Dave and watched the wheels going around in his head. He finished his almost true story about two weeks lying on a tropical beach.

"Sorry I didn't warn you. I do go walkabout sometimes."

Dave chimed in.

"Where in Redfern Nick? And what are we going there for?"

"Gary's place mate, next to South's Leagues club opposite the oval."

"Oh yeah, and who's Gary?"

Nick still hadn't told Dave about his plans for the future so he chose his words carefully when he replied.

"Just someone I want to introduce you to. Should be able to pick up the guys we need while we're there and he'll be somebody handy for you to know."

Gary's Place

SPLIT BY SYDNEY'S MAIN rail line and separated from the city proper by the breadth of a single road, Redfern has ever been a handy source of the blue-collar labour needed to maintain the workings of the city machine.

Unfortunately, in the early seventies, a federal government headed by an idiot named Whitlam, and best remembered for marvellous good intentions and stunning political incompetence, transferred the working class suburb into one of the most racially divided and dangerously violent spots in the nation. Public parks and footpaths became after dark no-go areas and even in daylight hours, for a single woman or aged pensioner, braving the streets alone became a peril-fraught adventure.

The one institution which continued to shine amidst poor old Redfern's socially bleak landscape was South Sydney Rugby League Football Club. A proud and noble club with history stretching back to the inception of the N.S.W. working class' favourite game, South's Leagues occupies a unique niche, as much a sporting icon as the Don himself.

It also supplied most of the glue which loosely held the fragile community together. So much a part of the city's fabric, in fact, that when Nick answered "South's oval, next to the ticket boxes," to the Bellevue Hill bred ex- accountant's request for destination, no further directions were required. Ten minutes after leaving Blues, Dave pulled the van to a stop in Chalmers Street, halfway between the club's front doors and the right angle bend in the road bordering the football grounds. Nick got out and led his travelling companions

to the front door of a three-storey double fronted Edwardian terrace.

Dave inspected the dark and silent front of the house, turned and suggested to Nick, "Might be out of luck mate. Midnight Sunday, doesn't look like anyone's home, or if there is they're all asleep."

Nick smiled and replied.

"Don't worry sunshine, there's about a dozen guys living here, there's always someone home, there's always someone awake. Gary's got a simple house rule, too, you don't train, you don't work, you don't live here, so they're all good value and there's always someone on tap. He's got a legal security company, does personal work himself, and hires the boys out to rock venues in the suburbs. Their heads aren't known uptown and I can get them for a reasonable price."

With that he reached for the heavy bronze knocker and rapped it twice, hesitated then three more times against its ornate base plate. He stepped back and peered up at the floor of the overhanging balcony. Within moments a timber panel lifted and moved aside to be replaced by a dimly seen shaved head and an English-accented "Shit! Nick! Good to see you mate," and louder to someone unseen, "Richard, get the door. Visitors".

The heavy door swung open to reveal a short dark foam lined corridor and a sweat-slicked young man dressed in a pair of boxing shorts. His face split in a grin as he extended a friendly hand. "Gees Nick, good to see ya."

Nick returned the handshake and replied. "G'day mate, why aren't you at work, you lazy bastard?"

He turned to his two friends and continued. "Coupla mates of mine, Bill, Dave, Richard."

Richard swapped grips with Dave's oversized paw and eyed the leather-clad blonde, as her hand met his he felt the obvious femininity and visibly relaxed.

Bill bridled, Nick chuckled.

"Easy girl, Richard, the D.J. at Rogues over in Darlinghurst, spends a lot of time on Oxford Street. Seems some of those girls with dicks have taken quite a shine to him. He's apt to be a little defensive."

The embarrassed D.J. released her hand and stammered out a clumsy apology.

"Sorry, sorry, no offence, the name threw me for a bit. Just I walk past 'bout a hundred guys a day who try real hard to look like you do."

Bill caught Nick's eye as she unzipped her leather jacket to reveal a tight white halter top, she traced her fingernail down Richard's chest to the waistband of his shorts, looked him in the eye and said, "That's okay Rick, I been there for the gay Mardi Gras. I can see how some of the boys would like a taste of you."

As his shorts bulged and his face flushed scarlet the embarrassed young man turned towards the thick sound curtain blocking the end of the passageway and choked an invitation over his shoulder.

"Aah, um, come on through," as he stepped into a leather and chrome furnished living room leading to an impressive open plan ground floor.

Bill and Dave stopped short in surprise.

In the centre of the room a polished and thickly carpeted staircase led to the upper floors while directly ahead the lounge opened to a scaled down boxing ring and a well equipped, mirror walled weights area. Beyond these stood a scrubbed refectory table and a modern kitchen. A door open in the rear wall revealed a compact laundry and the glass-walled backyard hot tub. The northern wall of the dining area comprised three glass-panelled sliding timber doors, at present in imminent danger of collapse as four snow white bundles of muscle and energy scraped, whined and head butted against them.

Chalky, his sister and two half-brother bull terriers had spotted a familiar playmate and they wanted IN.

Richard fled the length of the room to stand behind the waist-high kitchen bench.

Comfortably able to hide the results of Bill's practised tease, he offered drinks.

Nick paced partway across the room pivoted and smiled towards the couch to the right of the door they'd entered. Dave and the girl also stopped, their second surprise in a metre and a half, as an oaken-faced lion maned mountain rose to its feet.

The three-hundred-pound mountain of muscle bone and gristle expelled a great lung full of smoke, gently placed a seemingly tiny water pipe on the glass topped coffee table, stepped over it and grasped Nick's shoulders in spade sized hands, its thumbs met in the centre of his chest. Victor Spassky lifted his friend a foot and a half in the air and crushed him to his chest.

"Nicky, little brother, where have you been? I have worried for you!"

"Put me down you commie bastard, you're gunna break both me shoulders."

Victor put Nick back down.

"I am sorry my brother. There are people who would be happy if you were dead. This would make me sad. I have looked for you, where have you been?"

Nick looked at Dave and quickly considered what he hadn't yet told his partner.

"Bit of a long story mate. Haven't really got time to tell you 'bout it just now. Got some business. Is Gary home? And what are you doing here anyway? Oh yeah, sorry, these are friends of mine, Bill and Dave. Bill; Dave, my good friend and sometime major embarrassment Victor."

The Russian engulfed Dave's hand in his own.

"This is the boy who watches your back? His skin is soft. Are you sure Nicky?"

"I am sure Victor."

He turned his attention more directly to Dave and lifted the corners of his lips, almost a smile.

A silly man might have been insulted, Dave wasn't silly. Something told him grudging acceptance from this man was a compliment, the same thing told him it wasn't his size that made him dangerous.

Victor next turned to Bill, took her hand between thumb and two forefingers and brought her knuckles to his lips.

"Nicky has spoken of you, I am happy to meet you."

Just how his voice changed no-one really heard, but Dave suddenly pictured a brown bear inspecting a honeycomb. Bill's knees suddenly had a problem as, discreetly as possible, she chased Richard to the kitchen.

Nick punched Victor on the arm.

"Bloody Europeans, stop that!"

Bill took a glass of juice from Richard and laughed at Chalky's attempts to gain entry.

As she stepped towards the doors Victor answered Nick's questions.

"We go to work with Richard soon. Anna wants to see Rogues, she is upstairs making herself more beautiful. Gary is up in his office."

Nick's briefly held picture of his friend trampling various violent soccer thugs underfoot dissolved in his understanding of the Russian's all-pervading love for his sixteen-year-old daughter. After a messy divorce he had custody just one weekend per month and if she expressed a wish to spend a night with her father in Sydney's most exclusive upmarket nightclub, under age or not, that's what was going to happen. If Richard's status as the star attraction was insufficient to gain her entry, the doormen knew Victor. They weren't nearly silly enough to step in his path and say "no entry".

While Nick was digesting his disappointment, Bill decided it would be safe to slide open one door an inch to pat the dogs. Bad decision.

One inch led to a blunt nose, led to a block head, led to another block head, led to Bill flat on her back covered in pineapple juice as white balls of muscle and joy ran over, round, under and through her. Nails skid, slid, scrambled and finally caught traction on the tiled floor as four eager bullies changed direction and charged Nick.

He bent into a crouch and cried "Hi guys," as they bowled into him. Victor threw an arm over the worried Dave's shoulders and burst into laughter, Richard cracked up and fell about as Bill struggled to her feet spitting, swearing, laughing and searching for a sponge.

Arms, legs, paws, ears fur and tails tumbled across the floor in a welter of barks and yelps, to be answered by a roar from the floor above.

"Shut those bloody dogs up! Who let them in the house?"

Victor roared a reply.

"Shut up yourself you cranky dwarf, and come down, you have friends come to visit."

Victor and Richard grabbed two dogs each and dragged them outside by their tails, if dogs laugh, that's what they were doing.

The sound of a door closing and footsteps overhead, as Nick rose to his feet at the bottom of the stairs, Gary Pearce appeared at their head. Just Nick's height and a little more pudgy, Gary didn't fit the picture Nick's tone of voice had painted.

His current ranking amongst the world's top twenty professional kickboxers gave the lie to his appearance. They exchanged g'days and handshakes while Nick made introductions, then retired to the couch and water pipe as he explained the reason for his visit.

Ever the good host, Gary reached into a half full fruit bowl glued to the table top. He extracted a thumb of greenery, packed the water pipe's cone and offered it to Nick.

"Thanks mate but no thanks, I'll have to put my cranky head on shortly and get sharp. We're going to be outnumbered about two to one and that bowl of yours is always a bit of a lucky dip. Stumbling around with a head full of cotton wool and a heart full of love for all mankind just doesn't work for me when I'm trying to play gangbusters. Wouldn't mind a coffee though."

Gary had worked his way through from a pub bouncer in Brisbane's Fortitude

Valley to a respected reputation as a professional minder to the rock and roll world. After an argument with a local police inspector's son which left the arrogant, abusive prick with a permanent limp and the end to a promising career with the Broncos, that city's favourite footy team, relocation to Sydney seemed the best course.

He'd met Nick backstage at the Entertainment Centre the night he beat the visiting European champion and when he arrived back in town, in a rattley car with a bag of clothes, Nick offered him a bed for a couple of weeks and a handful of introductions. No slouch, within the year he turned the handful of introductions into a dozen suburban venues where he supplied quality security and jobs for upwards of fifty guys. Guys who knew what the job was all about, putting money in the tills, not inflating their egos by dragging some poor drunken idiot out the back and beating the crap out of him.

Most of the punters at these venues liked a smoke and expected it on hand. If one venue was a bit too keen in supporting N.S.W.'s archaic marijuana laws there were others which weren't. As the publican's licence depended on his public ignorance of such goings on in his place of business, it fell quite naturally to the security to set informal standards of behaviour and competition for the in-house trade.

They were well aware that adding the occasional joint to a pub full of rum drinkers prevented more fights than every doorman in the city put together. Consequently, considering its many sources, the quality of the backhand baksheesh that ended in the communal fruit bowl ranged from bush weed that induced a gentle glow and a warm smile to the hormone-pumped rapid growth hydroponic varieties that worked like a cricket bat to the forehead.

When Nick said "lucky dip," he wasn't joking. Coffee was definitely the better alternative and when Richard moved back to the kitchen to get it together, Dave saw a chance to improve the acquaintance and satisfy some curiosity. Bill wasn't slow, she figured her own curiosity would be best served around the mini espresso machine, so left the three serious heads on the couch to their own conversation.

JERRY THE POM

SINCE HE HAD BEGUN travelling with Nick, Dave had picked up a trick or two. With his own curiosity well and truly piqued and his mate's suggestion that these people were good to know, he considered his options. It spoke of the world in which he now lived that the first techniques to flit briefly through his mind were pure karate. Intended for suppression or punishment they involved the optimum delivery of his strength and power through a kick or punch.

The second file card to be considered and rejected by his skull-encased calculator was a series surgically selected from Brazilian jiu-jitsu and Russian sambo wrestling. Manipulations of limbs, joints and skeletal members usually resulted in verbal assurances and social behaviour precisely as required. Just like Brian's back bar, Dave was reasonably certain any display of physical jerks at this particular venue would only result in a three-month visit to a traction ward, or a serious dependence on the continued efficient function of an oxygen tent.

Silently embarrassed, Dave flicked his reflexive first options and plucked a third file card from his mental rolodex. Cynically referred to by Nick as psychology one on one, its pearls of wisdom were slowly gleaned from a six month study in behavioural science conducted on a bloodhouse door, it was "suggested" he work and a thorough reading of both Sun Tzu's two and a half thousand year old classic The Art of War and Dale Carnegie's sixties pop psychology paperback How To Win Friends and Influence People.

These pearls were then sorted and polished during innumerable rambling dialogues with his friend and mentor in the wee small hours. In Richard's case, a man who chose a career requiring his being up front and loud, the centre of attention, it all boiled down fairly simply - offer a compliment, stroke the ego and leave a gap in the conversation for the information to fill.

A complimentary query would probably be rewarded but, again like Brian's barroom, any probing questions would more likely result in a chilling silence, as cold and menacingly silent as the dark side of the moon. With a mental shrug ("nothing ventured nothing gained") Dave gave it a shot.

"Jesus Rich, what a house. I didn't think there was anyone home. That ghost on the balcony scared the hell out of me, then when we came through the curtain, shit, this place is amazing. How come you keep such heavy light and sound blackout at the front?"

Richard locked the chrome coffee filter into place, leaned back against the bench and waited for the heat to build. He looked the length of the of the open plan floor to where the heavy curtain hung, chuckled with dark humour and opened up an inch.

"Jerry's burglar trap mate."

Neither Dave nor the girl were happy to accept so bald a statement, the girl dug further.

"What's that supposed to mean? And what's so funny about a sound curtain?"

Now more relaxed with the imposing blonde, Richard considered breaking house rule number two {Whatever Happens In The House Stays In The House!}

Still, they were in the house, and Nick had brought them. Good chance to see if

her sense of humour was as dark as his own. He'd learnt early, when you wanted to unwrap the lady of your choice, humour seemed the best key. Strangely enough, once he got them laughing the clothes just seemed to fall off. Looking at Bill, like most men, he figured that was something he'd like a lot, and none of the guys resident would disagree with him.

Bill knew it.

Bill used it.

Dave sat back and watched her get just what she wanted for the price of a smile.

Psychology one on one could be most effective, but he was realist enough to

recognise where a horny young D.J. was concerned, it ran a distant second to a loosely wrapped, tight abbed confectionary like Bill.

He shut his mouth and opened his ears as Richard began.

"It's how a lot of the local thieves work. They'll go along the street knocking on doors. When someone answers or they hear someone inside they invent some bullshit story for knocking or just move on to the next house. There's a lane out the back, runs down to the back of the Leagues Club and they got a big dumpster bin. Walls along the lane are about ten feet high, triple brick. When there's no-one home they go 'round the lane, push the bin up against the wall and walk along the top to the place that's empty. After they do the house, if there's nothing in the backyard to get over the wall on they walk straight out the front door like they own the place.

Anyway, Jerry's really pissed off, reckons he didn't get his fair share of the last one, so he blacked out the front and cut that trapdoor in the balcony above it. He's got one of the front bedrooms on the first floor and you can hear the knocker real well up there. Reckons he's gunna jump on the next one, drive his head out through his arsehole. First one scared the shit out of Sally, You know that curly headed door bitch up at the Freezer? That's his girl, Sally, anyway, two days after the cops moved us in here, she's got out of the spa, asked me to put the dogs in the laundry for ten minutes and she's laying out in the yard in the sun wearing just a pair of knickers.

This junkie thief spots her, he's already up on the wall. See, no one's heard the front door, we didn't have that big knocker then, just a buzzer with flat batteries. He's thought, "You beauty," rob the place and get a fuck at the same time. She's jumped up and run in the house. He's jumped down and chased her. Mate, funniest thing you ever saw, the way the look on his face changed. I'm on the couch pulling a cone, Lester's doing bench press sets, he's pumped up like Godzilla, Gary and Ronnie are in the ring doing a Thai boxing workout, you know with the knees and elbows stuff, the McCoys are home, Mark's got his head in the fridge and Robbie's keeping time for Gary and Ronnie.

Jerry's asleep upstairs and there's another three guys upstairs on the bunks in the attic. This prick's got his eyes on her arse, doesn't realise there's anyone else in the house 'till he gets as far as the table there. Sally's pushed the laundry door open as she's run past so he's got Mark and the bullies behind him, the dogs aren't stupid, they can feel he's not welcome. Nearly fucking choked me. I've looked up, with a lung full of smoke, just as he's realised what's about to happen.

The look on his face, absolute funniest thing you've ever seen. I fell over, near shit myself laughing. By the time she's got Jerry awake and downstairs, he's charged down naked, that great cock of his nearly hitting him in the knees, never believed what the girls used to say about him 'till I saw that, anyway, he's too late.

Prick's out in the side passage, dogs chewing on him and six of us jumping up and down on his hands, ribs and knees. No point belting him anymore so we stuck a note on him, Jerry's safety pinned it to his dick for scaring Sally, and threw him back over the wall. We're laughing so hard it takes three throws, idiot keeps hitting near the top and falling back down.

The local Crown Sergeant that got us the house come 'round, reckons it took about an hour for the news to go right 'round Redfern. He wasn't too keen about the safety pin through the foreskin but no one got charged and there hasn't been a break in this end of Chalmers Street since. Neighbours are happy, Leagues Club's happy, cops are happy, everyone but Jerry. He spends his time, when he's not working, either meditating up next to that trapdoor or prowling about the rooftops in his ninja suit still trying to get what he reckons is his fair share. Keep telling him someone will shoot him, he just reckons

"Well, I am supposed to be this invisible ninjutsu teacher, if someone with a gun does see me, I deserve to be shot."

With a hiss of steam the espresso machine announced its readiness to serve.

Richard built a half dozen long blacks. When Bill put her hand up for milk he snapped jokingly at her.

"Don't insult my coffee you philistine, taste it and be amazed."

They'd quickly become comfortable in each other's company and the light-hearted banter was Richard's way of saying "pleased to meet you".

Collecting cups and a sugar bowl they wandered back to the living room and its three occupants. With caffeine, cones and cigarettes they'd settled about the room enjoying their particular poisons when Dave commented on the police connection.

"Brilliant house you got here mate, never heard of the cops being so fond of a security company they'd move you into their suburb, let alone into a place like this."

"Not so much the Redfern cops wanting us here as the Paddington cops not wanting us taking up their time.

Had a place over in Dillon Street, just next to the Scottish Hospital on Paddo's north side. Trendy neighbours kept calling the cops complaining about `barbarians` living in their street. Nothing they could pinch us over but between Lionel knocking a hole in one neighbour's bedroom wall with his dick, Jerry busting this sky waitress' arse and dropping a dead dog on its owner's doorstep, not to mention a fifty metre blood stain down the footpath they'd had about all Paddo could take of us.

Couple of the bosses came 'round off duty, told us about this place and suggested us and everybody else would be a lot happier if they didn't have to leave a car parked outside our front door. State Government cleaned up about forty houses around the oval, the Paddo cops put us in touch with the local Crown Sergeant and he teed it up."

Bill couldn't help herself.

"Who's this Lionel that knocks bricks out of the wall with his dick?"

Like Richard's "burglar trap" comment, Gary's spiel had again fired Dave's curiosity as well.

"While you're at it, if you don't mind, I haven't met Jerry but from what Richard was saying I thought he was straight and what's the story to dragging dead dogs around the streets?"

Gary looked at Nick and offered Dave a gentle reminder of just how popular questions could be. "Inquisitive buggers, these mates of yours."

Dave started to offer an apology.

"Ah, look, um, sorry if I'm speaking out of school."

Gary cut him off.

"No, no worries Dave, just a joke son just a joke."

He turned to Bill.

''Actually, Lionel didn't really knock a hole in the wall with his dick, but he might as well have."

"See, he always used to travel light. Bag of clothes, security licence and that's it. Pretty much lived on the road, touring with different bands. One night we're doing the after tour party for INXS, back when Kylie's trying to build some street credibility by being seen with Hutchence, and this obnoxious drunken idiot makes a `singing budgie` comment nobody appreciates.

Lionel gives him a slap and shows him the quick way down the stairs and out the door. Nothing special, but this record company publicist sees it and goes all weak at the knees. Next thing you know they're all in love and she decides to slow him down a bit by buying him this bloody great cast iron four-poster bed. Now Lionel likes a fuck, I mean he really likes a fuck, so while he's happy enough keeping a smile on sweetie publicist's face, cannot remember that girl's name, he's still spreading it 'round the groupies. So, 'bout a month after they get together, he's working a Psychotic Turnbuckles gig at Selina's down the Coogee Bay pub. That place gets pretty busy, they pack over three thousand punters in the room with only six guys working security. Not so bad when the bands are playing but between sets it can get awful ugly.

Anyway, band's doing a set so Lionel, as usual, figures he's got enough time and leads this star-struck teenager into the fire doors. They got this row of fire doors down the south wall, keep the outer doors to the car park chained and padlocked, not real appealing to the health and safety people but it does stop people sneaking in without paying and if you pull the inner doors almost shut it gives you a nicely private little cubicle, does get a bit hot in there though.

This is where things get funny, missed it myself but I musta heard this next bit from fifty different people. He's got this Turnbuckles groupie standing up, bent at the waist, hands against the wall, jeans 'round her ankles, giving her a good old horsie.

Click!

Someone's leant against the inner doors and locked 'em closed. Happens quite a bit really, we're forever finding punters who get in there for a joint or a quick blow job or some such, get locked in and nobody knows about it until we're closing the place and one of our guys checks all the doors. Lionel panics. Pulls out of the groupie and starts kicking his way through the doors. Timing's amazing, that karma shit Nick's always talking about, I'spose. Sweetie publicist's heard where he's working and come looking for him. Band's finished its set and the D.J.'s not ready, so except for this boom! boom! from the fire doors and some background chatter the place is quiet. It's a big boom boom, Lionel kicks pretty good, so a semi circle's formed 'round the door. Crash! down they come, he's kicked both doors off their hinges. Musta heard this fifty or sixty times. Sweetie's standing right there, groupie's still pulling her pants up, they're both lathered in sweat and Lester's still got his dick hanging out of his jeans, big oops written all over his face. 'Bout a thousand people watching, sweetie screams, stamps her feet and throws a mostly full bottle of Corona at him. Good hand speed Lionel, and not a bad talent for theatrics either; he plucks the bottle out of the air, pours it down his motor boat, smiles at her and burps.

"Thanks darling, just what I needed."

Fucking beautiful man, cracks the crowd up, not one more problem all night. End of the romance of course, but he kept the bed. Set it up in the Dillon Street house against a common wall, couple renovating the next door house have stripped all the plaster off their side, down to bare brick.

Lionel's got this aerobics teacher from City Gym up there and they've belted the top of the frame that hard and that often against his side of the wall it's knocked two bricks out the other side. They come crashing down on the woman's dressing table in the middle of the night. Police laughed about it but the neighbours weren't impressed at all."

Gary paused, leant forward and sipped from his cup.

"Good coffee Rich, just for that you can tell 'em about Jerry's contribution to getting us thrown out of Paddo."

Richard caught the ball and ran with it.

"If I'm going to be telling Jerry stories I want him in the room, don't want him complaining at me next time he's been partying too much."

He'd stood and walked to the foot of the stairs, "get down here you pommie git," by the time Gary replied.

"Come on, you know better than that, whether you can see him or not, he's heard every word said down here. Anything he's heard he didn't like he'd already let us know. Now get on with it and get to work you lazy bastard."

Richard returned to the armchair facing Bill.

"The dog was the last straw, so I'll start with the damage he did to the sky waiter's sex life."

He looked to Nick to guard his arse.

"You are taking him with you when you go aren't ya?"

Nick replied shortly.

"That's why we're here Rick, as long as he wants to come. Now you tell 'em the story while I work out who else is on tap and we can get going."

Nick's eyes swivelled in his head. Like a soldier on point or doormen in dangerous places, constant panning became so engrained it became unconscious as breathing until a sudden change or movement focused attention.

Three of the dogs remained pressed to the glass of the sliding doors, their attention fixed on the strangers while the fourth, Chalky, Jerry's dog, switched his focus to the island kitchen bench. Head erect and tail raised he suddenly stilled; as if on signal he quietened and sank to his haunches, a sign Nick had been searching for. He looked to Richard.

"Better still, we're losing time so why don't you go and get dressed. You're supposed to start work at one o'clock and Victor's said he'll join us at Heather's as soon as he's got Anna settled in the box at Rogues' with you. We've still got Kevin and the McCoys to collect so it would be better if these two hear about Jerry's fuck ups while we're on the road. He can tell 'em himself."

Nick had spoken his last sentence with a smile on his face Bill and Dave didn't immediately understand. He rose to his feet and turned to Gary.

"Thanks for the coffee and the line on the boys. Would you mind ringing Brian, tell him to get Heather to hold those arseholes inside until one o'clock. It'll take them at least quarter of an hour to all get outside. We'll be ready by then, promise, no more delays."

He turned to the back of the house.

"Hey, you, you pommie fuck up dog murdering poofter bashing rapist, you coming or what?"

The response from Bill and Dave was stunned surprise. Eyes gaped and jaws dropped as a cranky black clad wraith emerged vertically from behind the kitchen bench, a star shaped brass belt buckle rising a foot and a half above the marbled surface.

"Fuck you leprechaun. I'm no rapist and none of that other shit was my fault and you know it, and just how the fuck did you know I was here anyway?"

Jerry'd made his entrance. Not the one he'd intended but impressive nonetheless.

Nick replied.

"How'd I know? You don't really expect me to share leprechaun secrets with a ninja do you? Work it out for yourself sneaky, you move about as quietly as a bulldozer through bamboo. As for the rest, you can make your defence to these two while we're driving. Do it well enough and I might even give you the benefit of the doubt."

The tall Englishman had moved to Nick's side, clutched handshakes and exchanged shoulder slaps when Nick turned to his two stunned companions.

"Bill, Dave, meet a haemorrhoid I've suffered the last five years, Jerry. Jerry, meet two good humans, Dave and Bill. Let's get going."

Out the door, across the street and into the van, Nick's directions again were short.

"Selina's," was all Dave needed. Over his shoulder he addressed his black clad friend.

"Go on then, we got ten minutes to kill, tell these poor innocents how you got Gary thrown out of Paddington."

He spoke to Bill and Dave.

"Good warning for you two. Show you how jealous he can be about someone else's penis extension and what he's liable to do when someone interrupts him having a root."

From the moment he spotted Nick and company from his upstairs lookout, Jerry had been puzzled. Born in Brixton, he'd spent eight years in the British military, four of those years as a special forces trooper, before following his mother's "émigré" path to Australia. Trained and tasked to observe, analyse and report, inconsistencies and unusual behaviour had stirred his senses from the moment Nick arrived.

Everything Nick had done tonight had come under those two headings.

To arrive unannounced and in company was unique.

To encourage the stories of Lionel, a brother conspicuous in his absence, was unheard of.

Time was obviously a factor yet Nick was wasting it with hurried introductions and bonding chatter and now he wanted more of the same. He finished his thoughts with a trusting mental shrug, "Don't know what he's up to, but he's sure to come clean sooner or later," captured Bill's eye and meandered into his own defence.

"Seeing we're to be working together I expect I'd best address your senile companion's scurrilous remarks."

Nick interrupted. "Don't forget the dog, killer."

Without shifting his gaze, Jerry replied to Nick's taunt from the corner of his mouth. "Far less the alzheimer's risk than some I might mention, you whiskey-sodden drug fucked old bastard. Now just sit quietly in your corner and cherish what few clear memories you do retain, while I give these two charming young lambs a true picture of the events to which you allude. Care to hear an accurate version of events kids?"

As Dave bullied the bull-barred panelvan through a gaggle of hairdresser driven Hyundai's, Bill answered for them both.

"Wouldn't miss it for the world English. Sounds like a fun night."

She'd been enjoying the good-natured banter, up to the point of being labelled a lamb. A caustic retort had roared to her throat when, from the flashing light of a street light passing, she caught the twitch of lips that served Nick as a smile. The penny dropped. She realised they'd been presented for inspection, she realised they'd been subtly tested. Sensing she'd passed and been accepted should not have diminished her anger, but it did. Nick obviously gave this black-clad Englishman a wealth of respect. She was intrigued.

Dave was jealous. Picked up the offhand slur of racism, in Sydney's eighties an oft-used club to bruise public profiles, and used it to dim the Englishman's growing lustre.   It might have worked.

"You surprise me mate, wouldn't think an ex-skinhead bovver boy would be comfortable living in Redfern."

Jerry'd noted Dave's size, his age and his carriage, it was the first time they'd met.

When first he'd surfaced under Nick's wing Jerry'd looked at his history, couldn't figure why Nick took him on, a silly boy. Still, we all were once, perhaps he could learn.

Look son, when elephants fight, you can't survive in the middle of them. You've got to get behind one of them.

White, in Brixton in seventy three, middle of the race wars. What choices you reckon I had?

That's why mum come out here, every year more angry elephants. Dad dead, me in the army, she was too scared to go out of the house. Auntie Joan come out in seventy two, mum escaped in seventy five. Aussie army accepted my transfer in seventy eight. Bloody good country this one, long as you watch out who you got running it. That Whitlam for instance, where the fuck did you get him? 'Nother Churchill, Jesus, you people blind or what?

Oi! Bovver boy, you don't like it here I got twenty quid, you can take another whinging Pom home with you.

"Still living in the past eh midget? No bloody ten quid emigrant me, and anyway us Aussies talk in dollars nowadays, 'cept out Cabramatta of course, what's that now Baat?

Dave, sadly, still thought he was clever, and tried for some credibility.

"No mate, Dong, and yeah that is a worry, bloody Viet. Smack dealers. Should never have let them in the country."

Jerry caught Nick's eyes as they rolled up in silent apology.

When he'd looked he'd of course looked well, had some idea what might get his attention and sharpened his tone accordingly.

"Still don't get it do you, you dopey yid?' And paused.

"Feel that burr rising up the back of your neck? Called manipulation son. Yid, kike, Jesus killer, slope, dago, nigger, sand nigger, it's all the same. It's all people.' Less you're one of them religious lunatics that reckon everyone's gotta go to God today!, no-one wants his kids growing up hungry in a war zone. It's about poverty, it's about injustice, it's about power. It's about who's pulling the strings. Wealthy country, helicopters in the sky, scarabs on the rivers, Ferraris on the freeways. How come my kids need shoes? How come I'm working for ten bucks an hour? How come it hurts to pay the rent? Can't be the people running the place, they told me what a good job they're doing in their newspapers and on their television stations.

Must be the dagos over Marrickville or the slopes over Cabramatta, maybe the yids in Bondi or the abos of Redfern sucking us dry. Let's all hate them. Divide and rule son, cause consternation and conquer. Just how that disaster Whitlam got his snout in the trough. White boy me, from Brixton, no education. Wasn't 'til I got in the specials I twigged. Couple of young officers, third and fourth sons of Duke this and Viscount that, jumping through burning windows and ducking bullets, laying prone and living on cockroaches and stale water for weeks at a time. Kind of karmic payback for the cost of the families' appetites. Once in power no-one's going to share it. Long as the animals keep fighting amongst themselves no-one's looking at the keepers."

"No wonder you and Nick are mates, you're both crazy." Dave stopped trying, relaxed. Smart enough to hear he was being told something, the jibe got him more.

Jerry felt the tone, okay. "Not crazy mate, just been around long enough to see past the puppets. England it's institutional, here it's more personal. Look tonight. These guys gotta walk past three bars and two brothels to get from Peaches to Heather's. Not even slowing down. Someone's pulling strings".

LEARNING CURVES

BETWEEN THE PASSENGER AND driver's seats sat a broad and deep armrest. It had a hinged lid and nestled snugly within sat Brian's new pride and joy. Wonders of the burgeoning electronic age, brand new, military quality, tamper-proof mobile phone and high definition police radio scanner.

Dave's idea, while in truth born of his inability to stay silent for more than ten minutes, a dangerous habit soon quashed, and his boredom when posted on watch, the reasons he gave Brian to shell out seemed sound.

"How many times you wished you could get hold of the truck? Remember when Freddy's driver showed up with the money and the boys were already on the way. How embarrassing was that? Save the club shit loads on call centre Sal", a reference to the police communications centre sergeant who ran a discreet information service for discreet citizens. Expensive stuff, discretion.

"And isn't it better if he doesn't know what it is that you want to know?" That had been a bit of a worry, Sal had been running so long without an interruption suspicions had begun. Not stupid, the coppers. Could always be a smart move by the other side's smart guys to keep tabs on people in the know.

"You can get most of what you want straight off their own radios. It can have a secret number too. No-one needs to know it, not me, not even the driver just you, totally safe." While somehow Nick felt 'airwave scanner, radio telephone and totally safe' said altogether at the same time somehow didn't sound quite right, still, used properly it could be a good thing. He'd forgotten the conversation right up to the moment it rang a sudden shrill. Startled, thoughtful, composed, all quick as a blink, while Jerry's eyes bulged and Bill fell down from the roof he raised the lid and looked a question to the grinning driver.

"That's Brian, pick it up or just press that button on top and it goes to the speakers, he can hear us too, see, good." He was feeling clever again.

Nick pushed the button and Dave jumped in.

"Yes, boss."

"Hey, good! That's what I like to hear, teacher should listen to the student Nicky. Thirty years you still won't come to work."

Voice of vino domestico and hand rolled chop-chop over a bed of gravel, definitely not Brian's dulcet tones.

Jerry coughed a laugh.

"Shut up English, I shoot you."

"Fat chance you blind dago."

At their first meeting, two years earlier, one of the old man's slugs had missed Jerry by inches. A warning, a mistake, wrong man. Words were exchanged, people sat down, handshakes engaged, new friendships begun. As long as no-one's left dead, an OOPS! need not always be a bad thing. Now firm friends, the two did enjoy their dark intimate joke.

Dave's eyes snapped left, his hand moved right, just a flick, a shudder then right back on course, ears out, eyes wide mouth shut, thinking hard.

"G'Day Angel," gaze still on Dave. Conversation recalled, the certainty measured.

For differing reasons but like many before, Angel's voice had clubbed him. The surprise was complete, the recovery was smooth, a world well away from the last time his convictions were crushed.

Nick amongst few knew the story.

If Papa had sold pearls the world would have been Dave's oyster.

Papa didn't.

Papa sold diamonds.

Big ones.

Tall, athletic, dark-haired good looks, Midas touch and mind like a scalpel, the good luck fairy'd kissed Dave on the dick.

Yeshiva school was a breeze, Cranbrook a cakewalk, then off to the ivy-crusted, hallowed halls of Sydney Uni. for the commercial P.H.D.

A Porsche too gauche for the graduation gift, the more comfortable Merc. the go. Bondi west to Glebe Point South day after day to sit on his bum and absorb.

True, the girls liked the Merc. and the P.Patek watch but fat arsed and soft didn't seem to impress. For most of the city's trend setters, Oxford Street's dance clubs focussed the social, if you could wear spandex you were the star.

Sad stuff, but true.

Having been the star all his life, Dave knew just what to do. Exercise was needed, so a marvellously popular exer-box gym was joined. Not one to shirk work, nor waste a payment, Dave worked it hard. Six months later he's back in his spot, king of the club with girlies running off him like sweat. One night he walked out alone, encountered a world that he'd never known. Down the lane it lived, what once was a short cut, now locals knew better.

"Gis a smoke bro."

Four slim dark forms flowed around the dumpster, each a head shorter than Dave. Half drunk, smell of stale sweat and cheap wine. Easy beats all to a trained boxing giant. No problem.

"Don't smoke bro, don't have any."

"Not your brother you fucking white cunt, gimme ya wallet!"

These boys need a lesson. Two hours a day three days a week Dave had been honing technique. He flicked his fingers and loosened his wrists, folded his big hands into fists. Hooks off the front foot, balls of the feet, right jaw protected, left shoulder raised, jabs come crisp and right from the hip, footwork and speed by the bucket load.

None of which, he discovered, counts for jack shit when parties unknown smack you over the back of the head with a half full flagon of brown muscat.

Rich men for the next few days, they drank beer and ate chickens, bought gunja and smoked Winfield's.

Dave's take from the meeting lasted much longer.

Bashed, bleeding, stripped and splayed, POOF! 'cross the shoulders in three-inch cigarette burns, awareness shone dim when the neck of the flagon was jammed between his cheeks. Thankfully one of the boys noticed and jumped on his head. He was well back in the happy place by the time it was lodged with a place kick and bounced on the gutter to shatter. An hour more passed before the warm glow of lights from the front sliding doors of Sydney's C.I.B. beckoned. One hundred yards distant, quite a journey, one arm broken, unable to walk.

"Jesus, look at this piece of shit!" From the junior constable assigned to scan external security monitors. Too bad they didn't see across the street.

The Second Watch Commander stepped across to peer at the screen and watched Dave crawl hands and knees up the steps.

"Oi. Bit of empathy for our pillow-biting fellow citizens son, remember the lecture, you're in Darlinghurst now. Get someone out there, find out if it's been bashed or just on its way home from a party. Throw a blanket over it and call the Ambos, and get some bleach and a mop on those stairs, God knows what the filthy thing's carrying. And tell them to put on the gloves before they touch it."

Sympathy? What?

In and out of a coma, before news reached the family, no-one seemed to care. Helplessness and pain, shame, new things. A public ward is a lonely place.

Then the money came. Within six months the best of surgeons had removed all physical trace. The scars remaining went through to the marrow, his mind still shattered. Uncle Yossi came back from Israel, interesting character Yossi, he'd lived in the dark for years too long. He knew just where to find Dave's soul.

Took plenty of talk but they devised a cure. As always education first, then revenge, then a bedrock belief it can't happen again.

Yossi found Brian, Yossi found Nick.

Free financials and access to the extended family's legal advice.

"Got a lot of cousins in law, some of them judges" gained Dave a job at the club. Quiet conversation and a year up front sold Nick a student. The money up front bought him some bruises, the quiet conversation cut him some slack.

Naïve as a schoolgirl and brittle as glass when first they'd met, he'd come a long way.

Education he ate. Names, faces, facts and figures. Hand and foot techniques, individual and in combinations he soaked like a sponge.

The revenge wasn't right. His dancing partners from that black night had been found, and with Dave's eager participation, well admonished, but too much unfocussed anger still lived in there. Yes they could afford it and they were buying life lessons but Oxford Street girlies were not the right target. One of these days the contents of those rolex boxes should make a reasonable contribution to the Sallies. Feed some of the cold and hungry instead of bashing them. Oh well, long as there's not too many of us tonight should help a bit.

Confidence not right either. Chunks of arrogance through there. You can still see how he got himself bashed .Oh well, long as there's not too many of us, tonight should help a bit.

Keep telling you mate. Feet too small. No good for treading grapes me. Got anything else going? Wouldn't mind a little sit down job somewhere, some workshop with a view."

"How's that nephew of yours we set up in that shed out Granville way? Hear he's opened up over Dee Why now. Reckon he'd give me a run?"

"Ahh, I don't know Nicky. He's a big man now. Got them shops everywhere. All the kids now gotta have this juke box in the motor car. Can't go anywhere without a telephone."

Between a big bright moon and the short spaced street lights Nick watched appreciatively as Dave's cheeks began to redden. Mmm, good. He raised a quizzical eyebrow and measured the small postural changes as Dave's said "Okay I'm open."

"Wouldn't believe it, making millions selling tape recorders. Much too clever to listen to us anymore, he has new friends, more his age."

"Ooh Angel, no hubris, a terrible sin, would never have picked that, thought he was a real decent young bloke."

"A sickness Nicky, a terrible sickness, and most who suffer from it have no reason to. Contagious too."

Nick was fifteen when he met Angelo Savona. A very busy night. Ten years after an interesting war, which won him, amongst other rewards, a trip to Australia, Angelo was feasting on English as a new delight. A loquacious man, once you had won his trust; they'd spoken long hours. A secretive man, and thrifty, one word spoke three. Their familiar conversations left gaps in the lines.

"A bad one Angel, but not your fault, it can show up in any family."

"Too true Nicky, even the best."

Information was coming through, but slowly.

On a schedule, Nick pushed gently.

"Speaking of which, how is the best grape grower in Darling Point?"

"Pfft, him? He may be the father but I am their mother. He may boast of the vines but it is me with the fork and the shovel. So lazy Angel! he says. Nicky, we must have Nicky for breakfast, call him! Call him yourself! Busy he says, busy. What? An old man in the middle of the night. What busy? Lazy!

The harsh words melted to background as the gravel voice, as only gravel can, spoke of a friendship generations long.

"Breakfast? What? You old guys out of bed before lunch time?"

"Well that's the thing Nicky. We got this lunch, birthday party."

"Yeah, anyone I know? And how come I don't rate an invite?"

The jocular tone in Nick's voice met a wall of ice in Angelo's soft reply.

"Fulvia's boy, Mario, he's twenty five now. Fulvia and Frankie, some of his family, bit of a crowd really. Better day if the guests are spread out a bit."

Not a lot of time to spend, and Nick not keen to waste any, but Angel had knocked the top off a decades-old irritant. Nick pushed the conversation sideways, or so he thought. "Yeah now what the fuck is that? I don't think I've ever met the boy but every time I run into Frankie, and happy to say that hasn't been too often, his face goes red, steam shoots out his ears and he starts stamping his feet like his arse is on fire. What is that shit?"

"Same reason you haven't met the boy before, hubris Nick, jealousy".

"What?"

"You know the boy's second name?"

"No, but knowing Fulvia, I'll bet it's Tony."

"Anthony actually, and yes that was Fulvia's choice. She picked his third name too. Told Frank M.A.N. would be strong initials. Frank's never really paid her enough attention, I think he's always suspected she's smarter than him. If he tries hard enough it's something he can ignore. He knew the N stood for Nicholas but Mario was three before he realised where it came from. You know you might even run into him tonight if you're in town. His mother told him to be home before the sun, he's with his friends from the football. If you see him it would be good to remind him. She can be very loud."

"Happy to mate, if I knew what he looked like."

"Lionel, your friend Lionel, he knows the boy, they have met many times. A shame he is not with you."

"Never know mate, could run into him almost anywhere."

"Perhaps coming home from the beach."

"Yeah mate, perhaps. Either way I'll see you for coffee and some morning sun."

"And Nicky, your blonde friend, if she is not too tired perhaps she would like to come."

Connection broken, up past the hospital and through the lights, half turn to the right, they skirted the park facing the pub. Nick pointed to a car pulling out and gave Dave a prod.

He pulled to a stop and reversed into the vacant spot. As he reached for the ignition Nick stopped his hand and raised his index up across his lips, motioned to rev the engine and whispered in his ear.

"Roll down your window, when I open the back doors slide out as quiet as you can.

With the traffic noise and the engine running whoever he's got listening should think we're still on the road."

Nick unlocked his seatbelt, waved Bill and Jerry to the back of the van, placed his right foot on the seat beneath him, arched his back and lifted up through the passenger window. He took his left foot with him, half turned and placed it on the kerb.

As he finished his turn with a stride to the rear doors, a half full pub patron stumbled past.

Not sure what he'd seen, somehow it didn't look right, he stopped while his brain swam a lap, then turned to see the flying rubber guy talking to two giants and a blonde leather-clad dominatrix right there on the suburban footpath, about a metre from the van with the invisible driver. This was right up there with the talking dog he'd met going home about two weeks ago so he saved the price of the six pack he'd thought to buy and took himself home to bed.

By the time the drunk had started to turn Nick had begun answering Dave's raised eyebrows.

"Right. The old man knows where we are and what we're doing."

"He gives nothing away for nothing, coulda taught Machiavelli how to be sneaky.

Now he's told us he's got a bug in the car. And a tracker."

"How's that help him, where's his earn?"

"Earn" was a term new to Dave's lexicon. Once he learned it could mean reward other than money it became a question he asked a lot.

"Does love an earwig, the old manipulator, but information's only worth anything if you're the only one who's got it. There's someone else listening. Want to guess who that is? And why the old man's picked tonight to tell us?"

"The son?" from Bill.

"Gotta be," Dave posed his second question, two good ones in a row.

"What's that dumb prick up to?"

Jerry answered. "Gotta be the grandson. Jealousy? hubris?, where'd I hear that?

Anyway, he's Frankie's mate. Now we know how Frank feels, maybe the two of them don't mind spending the kid to drag the old man into this shit he's started with Brian. He knows Brian's got to attack them".

"Okay, we got business and Latin passion, gotta be a gun here somewhere, we need a couple of surprises of our own."

Nick went quiet, two looked expectantly, Bill mystified.

Nick delivered, turned to Jerry.

"After Angie's call, nobody'd be expecting to hear any more from you anyway, you may as well not be here. That skinny guy you had training on the post at home, reckon you could get hold of him?"

"Who? The guy with the long black hair, Brian?"

"Yeah him. Can you get hold of him?"

"He's working the Student Prince out Camperdown, he'd be keen for some serious shit."

"Bit mad?"

"Yeah, he's beaut".

"Okay. That wall outside Heather's, got that peaked portico thing over the gate, tall shrubs up the inside. Reckon you can get up there before we arrive? Looks like they know we'll be coming but I don't think they'll be able to see anything from inside the house."

Jerry nodded, already scaling the side walls.

"There's a cab base 'bout a hundred yards down the side there, use their phone and go get him. We'll see you there."

"No you won't, but we'll be there."

"Yeah, sorry mate."

Enough said, Jerry spun a pivot and loped his long legs around the corner then down the side of the pub.

"That's it, run ya faggot!" Rang behind him.

Nick was talking, Dave listening, but Bill took notice. Enough to see Jerry check stride for an instant before priorities overrode, enough to see the raucous young rugby player pull his head back in the window and leer at the glass-eyed student nurse he and his two predatory mates had primed.

The live-in girls at R.P.A. often used the Royal to soften the homesickness and meet people not smelling of bed pans and disinfectant. Occasionally one fell prey to such as these.

A dozen Jagermeisters under her belt, washed down with assorted beers, all supplied freely by her brand-new friends and little Miss Lithgow was already accepting a ride in the boy's panelvan to "Go look at the ocean".

Three steps from painful but unprovable memories.

Bill knew it, Bill saw it, Bill seethed.

"So, first thing possible, get hold of Griff. He's got a mate, Arty, runs the door over the Glebe pub. Ex A.S.I.O. Nowadays makes his main earn sweeping bugs out of offices for barristers and money jugglers. There's one in the phone for sure, for Ang to know we're out the beaches there's gotta be a tracker and you can bet there'll be a second mike somewhere. Keep the phone but make sure the thing comes back clean. Good bloke Arty, tell him I sent you, he'll do the good job. I'll get hold of Brian, let him know what's what and see if Angie's call has stirred 'em up. There's a pay phone in the bottle shop, just be a minute."

While Nick reached the phone and started to dial, Dave slid back in the van. Bill touched her stomach and pointed indoors. Dave chuckled at this female weakness, weak bladder for sure.

Bill started her stalk.

Edged down the footpath to the boofhead's window.

A long leather-clad left arm pierced the four sat on tall stools. Right hand and left knee braced against the exterior wall, the left hand cased in shot-filled fingerless glove took a good grip of dirty hair and shot the student stalker straight out in the street.

Nick had hung up. Heard the crash and the shatter and the screams.

The pound of lead shot sewn in the palm gave her shots plenty of power to shatter the thin facial bones. Cheek, nose and jaw gone in a trice. Silver-clad boot toes were doing bad things to knees and ribs when Nick yelled "Go girl, get!"

A short sharp sprint and a dive in the back. Twenty metres hard on the gas, just like he'd been taught, then hard on the brakes to slam the back doors."

"What the fuck!" from Dave as steam boiled out Nick's ears. Bill breathlessly offered defence as she convulsed in laughter.

"They were going to gang bang her! Ah shit, the look on his face before he got hit! Beautiful!"

"You fucking idiot! I've told you and you know it. You can't save the world, it'll kill you just trying. Just stick to the ones you get paid for, that'll be plenty. And we don't have the time. Why do think Jerry didn't waste the ten seconds to rip his head off?"

Not convinced, Bill sat huffy.

Nick turned his head to hide his grin and swept his eyes past Dave doing goldfish faces.

"Scary bitch, eh? Selina's!"

HEATHER AND BRIAN

THE SCENE IN BRIAN'S office was not all that different from Nick's prediction.

The principals were the same and it was payday but circumstances dictated that tonight's soiree take a more serious mein. Only one girl attended and once drinks were served and party favours dispensed, the black marble ink stand cleaned and gold tudes reset in their tricky fountain pen holders, Nicky was tipped fifty and pointed to the door.

As it closed behind her, Brian passed an envelope to each of his "guests" and edged around the desk to his oversize swivel chair. A big man, he and the desk half filled the room, he had had to take out a wall and rebuild it to get the thing in. While the two seated opposite sipped drinks, pinched noses and perused the contents of their envelopes, Brian spread his big hands across the desktop and allowed the memory scents of New South Wales western plains wash through him. Plus the acrid under taste of charred pork and soot.

Always painfully ironic, his father's desk, scene of so many childhood humiliations, all that could be saved of the family home. A rambling country homestead that grew from burlap and bush timber to cedar and stone as the generations prospered.

A pillar of the far-flung rural community, Dad made sure Brian received the proper education.

Agricultural college first then Sydney Uni. for that mixture of law and business preparatory to taking up the Federal House of Representatives seat handed down when Dad retired. A rugby scholarship the perfect vehicle. With rural politics today as medieval as the doomsday book this seemed the perfectly natural order of things. Life progressed as the seasons.

Like any other Aussie country boy, first time off the farm and possessed of bull thick bones, goanna-catching speed and a one hundred and ten kilo frame, Brian made the most of his rugby days. Didn't mind the dancing girls either.

He was packing for his first tour, South Africa. Not yet a named team member but just one turned ankle from a run on player and the long-sought social elevator Wallaby jersey a reality.

He was happy right up to that moment.

A knock on the Potts Point apartment door revealed the team manager and two Federal Police.

Caused him to confront motivations, to question it in others, to lose it in himself.

Denise, the long-term Canberra assistant, had arrived unannounced at the family manse.

A bump in her belly and a long denied thirteen-year-old on her arm.

Other than him the whole family was home, Mum, Tess, her husband Wayne and their two kids, younger brother Tom and his current Melbourne model girlfriend.

Way too embarrassing for Dad.

He shot the lot.

Packed diesel and phosphate, spread petrol about, stood in the middle with a match.

The office was locked and out in an upwind wing. The desk survived.

Brian didn't make the tour, he had a drink instead. Found the family name had suffered a cloud, polite society no longer called. He recalled the dancing girls and took to the streets. Six months later he had become well known as a patron not wanted. An angry drunk giant is seldom welcome in the same bar twice.

He'd damaged half the strip's doormen and cost a lot of business by the time Nick was asked to look.

"Next thing's to shoot the big prick but it would be better if you can do something about him."

He was pleasantly surprised the angry ex-front rower's eyes, nuts and chin weren't that much more resilient than many others he had met. This gave them the chance to chat. The big guy surprised Nick again. By his ability to speak, by his ability to think, by his ability to weep. By his ability to pull out his thumb, head back west and settle his demons, but most of all by his ability to reappear twelve months later and buy the number one rock and roll night club in the city.

Like any good student of Sun Tzu he'd done his homework and the place went from strength to strength.

The staff were happy, the punters singing and dancing and the tills
   a'jingling.

A good bloke, Brian, most cheered his success, bringing new friends and family, but some brought resentment and greed. New enemies arose, some subtle, some not so.

A lot of Police played rugby.

A lot of Police studied law.

A lot of Police liked the calm status quo.

Tony and crew sometimes kicked a soccer ball.

Tony and crew fought the law.

Tony and crew sought bloody revolution.

Both hard street coppers in their time neither MacCauley nor Thompson won rank through stupidity.

They knew what their political masters wanted, certainly not embarrassing headlines like "Mob wars in street!"

They knew what they wanted.

The pay packets were regular and fat.

Brian got them box tickets for the Bledisloe.

Brian was fighting for his life.

Motivations coincided.

Formalities settled and thoughts collected, attention turned to the matter at hand. The conversation had well advanced, had already passed the "There are no organised gangs in New South Wales" part when Nick's call interrupted.

With no disagreements in the room and everyone in play, Brian switched to his new speaker phone.

"Got a couple of mates on the line."

"Yeah good, if they're your regulars we can use some input." Nick quickly explained the information leak, leaving out Angelo's curious part. No need for police, however well paid, to hear his name.

When the State Premier famously declared, at the opening of Kerry's entertainment centre, "N.S.W. has the finest police force money can buy," he hit the nail right on the head.

For the right money you could buy whatever information you desired. When motivations coincided they might even provide some services.

Brian paid well and often.

He put his first question to the plain-clothed Thompson.

"Okay, you're Mr. Intelligence, where's that put us?"

"What's this 'us' shit, white man? Our team don't fight your wars."

"Those pricks win this thing, take me out, it'll be your war then. You know damned well what their go is. Cars, armed robs, speed, smack and guns. Six months and you'll have teenage would-be`s wired on gutter drugs running automatic weapons up and down Darlinghurst Road. That'll make you popular. That little blonde Fed they snuck in as a waitress, you gotta be getting her reports. Every bloody wall and partition in the place has got a Chinese Kalashnikov inside of it. They're building an armoury. You intend doing anything about it before they start selling them, or using them?"

"We know where the guns are. We don't know where they come from. That's why she's there. Until she gets the source the Feds will do nothing. If they start pulling them out and putting bullets in them, she gives us that call, okay, I can run a couple of teams in. Until then you're on your own."

"What do you mean 'Gives us that call?' She walking around in there wired up? They spot that she's fucked."

"Well, no. That Tony really is a dead-set goose. She walked into the interview and straight up told him she's a cop. He's that far up himself with his yellow Ferrari and gangsta bullshit he's believed she wants in. She's fed him a couple of warnings when we were going to raid one of his cut and shunt shops, told him they were things plucked out of radio traffic. Timely, let him move his head guys and most of the stolen shit out before raided. Worked well, we got to watch where it all went. She's had a couple of lines, even fucked one of the cousins. He thinks it's funny having her walking around selling drinks and dope with a cop radio on her hip. Stupid? If not for his old man he couldn't get a job at McDonalds.

"Well, present company excluded of course, I have met some cops quite fond of money, and one or two dippy blondes. You sure she's still on side?"

"Something Tony don't know, the whole job was her idea. She had a little sister, died from a heroin O.D. In the toilets, in the Hole. They dumped her down Woolloomooloo behind the Frisco. She'll do anything to find the guy who stuck it up her nose. Tell ya, that good looking cousin's lucky he didn't get his dick bitten off. If she's changed sides I'll stand fucking in the front window of David Jones Saturday morning."

"Well that's good. She's inside, she's on side, and she can talk."

Brian turned his attention to the poorly disguised MacCauley in his sweater- covered uniform.

"Where's Serpico?"

Referring to the offbeat but straight-arrow drug squad detective who revelled in mimicking his American role model.

"Is he still taking pictures of the doormen?"

Thirty metres from his prey, Detective Senior Constable Greg Townsend lay in the gutter. Wrapped in tattered, metho-soaked rags, he played the street sleeping homeless alcoholic to perfection. He made a point of urinating on his plastic-lined costume before each shift. The heady reek of metho and ammonia kept both tourist perambulators and predatory locals at sufficient distance to hide the quiet whirr of his automatic camera.

The arrogance of the bosses ran right through to the steroid-pumped boys on the door. They plied their trade openly beneath the bright entrance light. A club patron, from time to time, would stick his head out and exchange cash for a capsule. More often a passer-by, some nervous, some familiar, would strike a conversation, invariably ending in an exchange for his or her poison of choice and an untidy sprint back to the waiting needle.

With dozens of frames recorded of low level flunkies doing their thing, even a bashing recorded to be produced at an appropriate moment, Greg waited the link shot.

Estimates were the boys were doing over seven grand a night. That much money had to go back inside and that much dope wouldn't be kept in pockets or behind the door bitch's desk.

A firm believer in karma, senior Townsend had no doubt a few more nights of this piss- soaked purgatory would give him his prize. The next link in the chain he knew led to Tony.

Someone to be quietly collected, quizzed, threatened and released on a leash.

"What's with those two, problem's down at Heather's, not the Hole".

"When these boys step out of Feathers I want them well fucked and lazy. I'm going to be standing right in front of 'em. They'll be counting on me showing up, but if they hear there's a posse outside they'll come out like Butch Cassidy and the Sundance Kid. They're gutless pricks when it comes to punching on, if they're warned they'll come out guns blazing."

"Not even Tony's stupid enough to think his phones aren't tapped so whoever he's got listening has gotta send a runner, then he's gotta send a runner to Heather's, probably more guys as well. I need your girl inside to tell us who he's sending. Then there's three ways you can go from here to Heather's, I need Serpico to tell me which way. One other thing, they've left the bus up Victoria Street near Peaches. Nick wants it outside Heather's front door, give 'em nowhere to run. It's quiet down there, Nick'll get the lane blocked but I'll need a couple of your guys up on Macleay Street to direct people around the gas leak."

"What gas leak?"

"The one that makes it necessary to keep people out of there for about twenty minutes."

"Oh that gas leak. They can be expensive, can gas leaks."

Brian opened the left hand desk drawer, pulled out a rubber banded monkey and slid it across the desk.

MacCauley scooped it up, murmured something about grateful beat cops and tucked it into a trouser pocket.

He was quick, MacCauley, but greedy. Both Brian and Thompson knew full well the footsore street patrol would be lucky to see any of it. A small squirm and fidget showed Brian that Thompson didn't sit comfortable with his partner's opportunistic theft. Teams were teams and the Fed was unlikely to back a civilian's complaint against a colleague. Still, another small sliver of the slow moving jig-saw that had become Brian's life. Store it away and remember it, like a plumber throwing that unused washer into his toolbox, it could come in handy some day.

He opened the right hand drawer and pulled two police issue radios out of their charging blocks, looked up across the aged timber and quizzed his expensive guests.

"What channels are they on?"

"She's on eight, he's on eleven. "Okay, I'll let Heather know what's happening and get her to turn off the phones for an hour. He just might get someone to ring. You get on the blower and let yours know what's got to be done."

While the two guardians of society slipped quietly out the back door to their parked car and communications, Brian pulled in the jolly jokers from his own front door. G.I. Justin the Motown refugee and Mighty Mick, life support system for the massive moustache. Some idiot decided to pull it one night. Sad what happened to his life.

As socially philanthropic as ever, Westpac had thoughtfully provided a financial safety net for young immigrant Polynesians caught temporarily between employment. To the right, across from the club, at that edge of the open red paved mall, where shadow met light, sat two automatic teller machines. A corner where young cousins from Tonga, Fiji or Samoa might meet to reminisce, have a chat, have a laugh, go fishing.

Perhaps invite an unsteady cash-renewed tourist into their comforting shadow, lay him sleeping on the slightly more red pavers and relieve him of his heavy financial burden.

"How many boys working the bank?"

"Three, you want them moved?"

The cousins, like any clever hunters, had learned not to put too many fishermen along the bank, lest they frighten the fish.

"No, no. Reckon we're going to have a runner come past from the Hole in a minute. He needs a little lie down."

"What are we, lace curtains?"

"No, you're big loud scary arseholes who like the dills down the street watching while you smash people out the front here. I want them to see this guy go past still walking. I'll let you know when he's coming, you tip the boys. They're sure to have a couple more mates tucked around here somewhere."

He produced a worn fold-up polaroid camera and a hundred dollar bill.

"Give one of them the camera and the spot. When he comes back with the camera and a picture of the guy sleeping there's two more. And tell him don't forget to rob the guy."

"Mate, time he wakes up he'll be lucky to have any clothes left."

Brian chuckled. "Yeah, okay. Now get out there and do something for all that money I'm paying you. I got calls to make. It'll be any minute."

He riffled the refidex and dialled a number. The ring on the far end, a public booth fifty metres from Heather's front door, stirred Blues from his vigil.

Could tear your heart and pull tears from your eyes with a harmonica could Blues. Also quite happy to take teeth from your mouth with his steelcaps.

"Yes?"

The tall wall, the taller shrubs, the portico with its light and the artful "Feathers" in brass script atop the bellpush, Heather's business looked exactly what it was.

Reputation conscious citizens parked their cars elsewhere, Brian checked anyway.

"Anything parked out the front?"

"No."

"Where'd they leave the bus?"

"South of Peaches, 'bout halfway between the pub and Tony's."

"Want it down outside Heather's, box 'em in, anyone watching it?"

"Left a driver in it but it's out of sight of Tony's."

"Need a hand?"

"No, no, I'll be right, take about twenty minutes."

"No rush, Nick's still out in the sticks, he'll be a while yet. I'll let Heather know and sort a couple of bits here. When you get there stay in the bus, I'll be down in about twenty minutes."

"See ya."

Blues hung up the phone and began to retrace his footsteps.

Heather was reaching for the handset when Brian's next call arrived.

It had taken her less than five minutes to pick the boys as more than motley crew. Another twenty of charm, flattery and auspicious partnering gave her the space to slip into her hidden office and sound the alarm. Brian's call caught her mid-stride.

He quickly filled her in, then "Tell the girls to work them well, we'll be outnumbered so wear them out a bit."

"Most of them are drunk already, but there are three of them that might be a problem. Wouldn't take a room, or a drink. They've got two girls in the lounge making coffee and chopping lines. When I told them to pull up, one of them pointed a thirty eight at me and told me to fuck off. I don't like him."

"I don't like guns. What's he look like?"

"Easy to pick, the three of them. Older than the rest, big, one in a suit, this one's in a leather jacket and jeans."

"Thanks, best cut the phones in case he does ring. I'll let you know when we're lined up outside."

"How?"

"Easy, their bus will call them."

"Don't rush, after what they did at Peaches the girls will be happy to help."

Channel eight said "Four and leaving now, repeat, four and leaving now," then fell silent.

While the tightrope walking undercover cop bent to her duties, give another punter a real good look at her teats and talk him into the most expensive drink in the place, Tony sent two more.

The four passed the door and turned North on the dogleg avenue. Twenty metres and they split at the veering lane, two high profile to pass Brian's front door and two to step past that pile of stinking rags and slip quietly through the car park out back.

The pile of rags hit the transmit button and spread the news.

From Brian then to Justin who with hand signs and head nods told a young hunter there were two and asked if help was required. The happy Samoan smiled no thanks and floated down the dim lit street. Several deeper shadows seemed to follow.

Next to stand Phil from his comfortable stool.

"Got two guys coming 'round the back from the Hole, need to disappear them for a while."

"How long?"

"Coupla hours."

Phil looked relieved. "How about a bin? That's quick and easy."

On the thriving tourist strip refuse was a problem. Restaurants had gone for back lane dumpsters, and Maccas was a beauty. Wide, long and not too high, you could flip the plastic lid open with one hand, dump your rubbish and be gone in a jiffy.

"Yeah that's good. Let Kevin go first, see if he hits like Stevie said." Kevin had won his job on recommendation, so far no-one had seen him in action. Phil hustled through the back door to cue him.

The dancing girls went ears up. They read body language better than most and sought to earn some points. When the message boy Favios emerged from the lane they were mobbed. While the front door of the Hole was always open to the girls between shows, these were exactly the type of shithead that had them clamouring at Brian's back one. Warm hands and salacious whispers turned their heads.

"Got a line for a blow job?"

That held their attention while Lionel and Phil slipped closer.

Not terribly well educated, Kevin knew jack shit about Bruce Lee's Chinese one inch punch. What he did have was the South Auckland six foot right hand. He used it to gymnastic effect, made big bad men turn cartwheels.

A deep throated "Ho Ho Ho" drifted down the lane as Phil's meaty palm contacted the other messenger's chin. He lay down next to Kevin's friend.

An easy heave put the boys in a bin, the girls walked inside.

Tony's last two, sent late, went west from the door. Training partners, they hit Victoria Street and headed north in an easy jog.

A hundred metres from the approaching Blues they passed beneath a street light. Gold chains and tracksuits, arrogant laughter, no mistaking these boys, or where they were heading. Blues spied about, a muddle of old masonry in the front of a newly renovated terrace. He selected his kiln dried club and waited, knees bent behind the front garden wall. Ears were enough to gauge their approach.

Two paces distant and closing when he swung gate-like from the fence and drove

a four pound federation brick straight into Claudio's mouth. While he dropped quicker than the brick Roberto snapped into a sprint. Two against one he'd be happy, one against one, not so keen. Besides, he didn't really like Claudio all that, much and he did have a message to deliver. He was right to run, he told himself as he passed the fifty metre mark.

Blues watched the young gazelle disappear into the dark. No way his tired old legs would catch him. Hoping he'd done enough he headed towards the bus and its unsuspecting driver.

THE McCOYS

ROBERTO, STILL PANTING, PUSHED the brothel bell twice, Blues eased the bus into gear, as Nick pointed South off Coogee Bay Road.

"Take a right for a couple, then left, come down past the Oceanic and put it in the car park."

The Coogee Bay Hotel. Built on a huge corner block straight across the park from the surf, the Coogee Bay played host to a wide community. Surfers and bikers, footy players and flat out drunks mingled and mixed with happy families and searching singles. Four star beach front accommodation, good food and four big bars. Then there's the beer garden. A half acre expanse of grass wrapped by the horse shoe driveway with comfortable outdoor seating and edged with a dozen majestic old growth palm trees. For lunch and a beer, for a steak in the sun, idyllic. A dozen tall and wide local league players, one taller and wider part time debt collector and smiling, soft spoken Australian heavyweight boxing champion maintained the ambience.

Then there's the night club. Where the ambience turned to sex, drugs and rock and roll. Just about the biggest live venue in town. Wide-bellied with a cathedral ceiling, the stage set five foot high for good viewing, a line of fire doors lining the south wall for safety and a twenty metre bar. Licensed for twenty four hundred patrons, at fifteen dollars a head a promoter could make good money over a three night weekend. Of course if the pub kept the fire doors chained and padlocked to prevent punters sneaking friends in for free and you packed another twelve hundred dancing drunks up on the mezzanine no-one seemed to notice, you could make even more. There's the security of course, but if you cut that to just six guys you can save thousands of dollars. The six guys weren't too keen on this policy of course but sliding in certain friends, students and dojo training partners they could often build a handy undercover intelligence net.

Tread on any unconscious punters? Where?

Who's selling what to whom? In what corner?

Where's the next fight going to start? How many?

And a physical back-up for when, as always, they found themselves out numbered.

Dave paused the van at the corner, allowed a moment's empathy for the near empty, hopelessly outgunned opposition pub, then turned left and let gravity pull them down the hill to the south end of the horse shoe drive.

Thirty-odd Harleys stood near to the footpath in line. Two cranky pledges, beer can in one hand, joint in the other, left to stand guard while their patched would-be brothers grew drunker and louder on the grass expanse.

As they bumped across the driveway to take the narrow spilt down the side of the pub to the night dark car park, Nick gave them a thought.

"There's trouble waiting to happen. Want to get out of here before that erupts."

Since the lack of lighting made the car park more popular with muggers than staff "Don't leave a car out there unless you're willing to fight your way back to it," there was always plenty of space.

So they locked up and headed to the front, Nick queried Dave.

"Who's running the show now Noel's fucked off to the States?"

"Joe, Joe Cirinno."

"Who?"

"Joe, that young bloke that came up from Melbourne for the two Nicks tour. Remember? Barker and the Reptiles and Nick Dreads with Wolfgang. He bashed some Painter and Docker's son down in Lygon Street. Good idea to get out of town for awhile. Door bitch spotted him and he's been here ever since."

"What? Katie the star fucker. Thought you had to be a lead singer or the promoter to get a look in."

"Yeah well, he does lack a little local knowledge and does like to keep a low profile but the girlies love him. Good looking, silver tongue and can fight. Happy to step out three or four at a time. You know what that does to 'em, bit of sweat and blood. Gets some nice coke too."

Nick laughed, "Funny that, how a coupla grams of marching powder effects a girlie's knees."

"Knees?"

"Yeah, they either drop to the floor or go straight to the shoulders."

Bill bristled, "You know you can be an arsehole sometimes."

"Just getting into character girl. Lotta bikes out the front. If we're not out of here chop chop we're going to get caught up in something ugly."

"You gone mystic again? Telling the future?"

Nick twitched, head, shoulders and eyeballs flashed a whip. Dave flinched, "Look, accountant, count. How many patches you see? How many members you reckon at the tables? Two sets of colours drinking jugs together. They usually share jugs by bashing each other over the head with them. Eight tables, half a dozen of each couple floating. That's about fifty to me. I reckon about thirty bikes. That's about twenty patched members riding sissy. Bullshit. Betcha the rest of the bikes are somewhere near. They've doubled up for a quick escape. And we've just walked straight through their line of sight of the garden bar. You had a look at Bill lately? Bright back lit? Not one fucking word. Something ugly."

They reached the three long shallow steps that fed patrons to the club's four front doors. One set each side for entrance and exit. Two set in the centre with a common push bar lock, very handy for hurling transgressors straight out the venue. While most drunk punters accepted their ejection with bad grace, they accepted it nonetheless. Occasionally, and not hard to pick, one would bounce back with violence. For these some inept builder had placed a most handy bouncer's aid. Dead centre of the double doors, about a metre out, stood a fluted iron column, faint spots of blood spatter still stain its inner face. Spat out the push bar doors, half nelsoned arms and appropriately aimed, a convenient oops can be easily arranged. Stopped a lot of fights before they got started, Clive the Column became a popular member of the small tight team.

As the mismatched trio stepped past Clive a figure broke from each of the side doors. Robbie from the right.

"G'day Reeboks."

A merchant seaman and fond of a quid, Robbie learnt early that a sex, drugs and alcohol blow out after three months at sea can cost thousands. The brothers were building a little house up the coast and big brother Mark had no hesitation beating him over the head with a stick if he came up short on the mortgage. He found his answer at the boutiques of Bangkok, made a point of topping up his 'personal items' each trip. Quite lucrative, the mark ups on $5 polos, $60 rolex and $20 reeboks. For doormen trained to use feet like fists, the change from heavy long lace-up Docs to lightweight pump-ups was a welcome relief, especially after an all-night shift. The fall apart polos and slightly rust-resistant rolex went to drunks with an eye for a bargain. Mortgage got paid, Robbie got drunk, everybody happy, earnt himself a nickname as well.

"Nick! Cranky old bastard, didn't expect to see you working here again."

"Not working mate, recruiting, got a monkey for an hour or so's work, you interested?"

Every now and then Nick would ask a question he knew the answer to.

"Fuck yeah, when?"

"Now, and where's Mark? I want him too."

"Be back soon, he's gone to get the truck."

"Ah shit, he's not packing it is he? Don't have a lot of time to waste."

Mark had started working life early. Second of three sons to a soon single mother, by aged 12 he was working the crowds at the speedway. Selling ice cream and coca cola from a neck-strapped plywood tray, he soon learnt the value of a quid. He also learnt there were thieves in the world. To some in the crowd, filching coins from the skinny kid's tray looked like candy from a baby. He added two carefully broken coke bottles to the back corners of his tray and from then on hands that snuck in greedily retreated fast, loud and bloody. Occasionally, for the first couple of months he'd take one on the nose. These moments became crowd favourites. No matter the action below, the hill side crowd would turn all attention to the skinny red head kid as he picked someone to guard his goods, drew his jagged attitude adjusters from their back corner nooks and advance on his would-be thief. None took the challenge. With hearty crowd support, apologies were often accompanied with a fist full of folding. Having completed his studies in food and beverage, asset management and money for violence, Mark moved on. The hot dog bins next outside of the footy. A lucrative enterprise and popular spots were hotly contested, again food and violence sent him home flush.

Uncle Harry put his hand up. A long term MWU rep, under siege and starving with the demise of national shipping, he still possessed the leverage and knew enough about buried skeletons to gain placements for his two favourite nephews with Tasmania's Maritime College.

Freezing nights and school room days and before you knew it both boys merchant seamen. Long swings to distant and exotic ports with month-long layovers in between. Robbie filled his off days with Jack Daniels and dancing girls while Mark upgraded his first love, a converted F100 with a warmer for pies, ice for drinks and racks for sandwiches.

A twenty-two-year old with a halter top and hot pants to charm carpenters to the footpaths from smoko to lunch. Credit was allowed and between swings Mark drove. While hot pants flirted, Mark put his hand out, tax-free income, Mark loved his truck.

"No mate. He's picked up this fuckin' huge bull bar from the council auctions. Got Phil over at Randwick to fit it, just gone to pick it up. Be back soon."

A curly-haired figure with a wide bright smile stepped from the left hand door. A nod to Dave, a wink to Bill and a warm hand shake extended.

"Nick! Good to see you. How'd you know about this? The pub call you?"

"Joe, G'day mate. Know about what? The bikers? Know nothin' mate, just got here. Got a little a problem in town, come to collect Mark and Robbie. Not that I really want to know, but, what's up? Not good when these arseholes aren't attacking each other, means they're after someone else. Not you is it?"

"No mate, not me, it's that's fuckin' idiot manager out of the garden bar. The clubs were right on the verge of a speed war. Pledges were already putting bullet holes in each other's houses, so the presidents and sergeants arms had a sit down out here. Fuckwit got scared just having 'em here. Got Marley and big Tony to pull out one of the presidents and find out what's happening. He saying nothing of course, so, just because he's an egotistical prick, he's king hit the guy they're talking to. Broke his jaw. Gutless prick hasn't been to work since. They've been here every night. Bit of a worry."

"Yeah, true. It is a bit of a worry, but the good thing is it's the pub's worry, not yours and mine. As long as they stay sat still 'til Mark gets back and we're out of here I'm happy. If they blow up after that, just close the doors."

"Yeah, then we've just the shitheads inside to deal with. Mark won't be backreal soon, you got time for a walk through? Don't know why, seems like we're fighting a dozen times a night. Place has changed mate, lot more violent since you left."

"Don't be fooled son, it never changes. Whenever ten thousand arms and legs get together, there's never a brain, just herd dynamics. Like fish mate, or sheep. You don't have to belt all of them. Or even control them all, just the ones the other are looking at. Call it crowd control. Stroudie's the best at it. Over in Perth. Saw him once move five hundred punters from one end of the bar just moving his head."

"Bit far to travel for training."

"No one expects you to be that good. Don't worry, there's plenty of people in Sydney know about mass manipulation. You ever work with that prick Garrett out of the Oils, you watch him close. Hate to admit but he's damn good at working herds."

"He was the reason you and Lionel quit wasn't he? What happened there?"

"Fucks me mate, I still don't know what he was up to. Self-centred power hungry hypocrite prick."

"Jesus you really don't like him, do you."

"No mate, smart bastard, but he has done it well. Steps out at Balgowlah Plateau and Sydney Uni and beats steel workerooh Barnsie to the 'voice of the people' tag that every Aussie loves. You and me and social justice. Fucking genius, you watch, he'll end up a millionaire car dealer or a politician."

"What happened?"

"He played the crowd. Don't know why. Maybe practice, maybe just for fun. He turned them all against us, gave us a hell of a night. Twenty or thirty fights in the next few hours."

"How'd you piss him off?"

"Didn't mate, I reckon it was a set up. Andrew got us together before the gig, told us that orders from the band were that no one was to touch him. Not one hand. Anyway, it's a high stage so when the girlies get a boost up they're easy to see and slow coming. I put Lionel and John the Ewok on one side and me and Coconut on the other. Took it turns when they get a boost, one of us would run out, catch her round the waist throw her across the shoulder, across the stage and back down to the crowd at the edges. Good fun actually, no one hurt, done it a dozen times before. Anyway, about ten minutes before he stops the gig he starts putting us on the Nazis, evil examples of social suppression, getting between him and his beloved fellow citizens. Three and half thousand drunks, half of them wired and all on their toes, he points them at us then wiz zip he's out the back door and off. Five in the morning we're up at Benny's drinking sake and pouring it over split knuckles when his stage manager and roadies walk in. Boys wanted to bash the lot of them, me too actually, but no Garrett. Sat them down and had a chat instead."

"No, no, he don't come drinking with us. Finish and home for him. He'll start a riot anyway, he doesn't give a fuck, as long as he looks good doing it, and suffers no consequences he's happy. Fuck us, you and everyone else."

"Watch him, he's clever, but do it from a distance."

They entered the room and conversation ceased. With the Psychotic Turnbuckles playing and slam dancing the fashion, words were drowned as they left their mouth, hand signals the go.

Joe signed and led through the crush, across the floor and up the wide staircase to the mezzanine. They topped the stairs and arced right across one horn of the wide horse shoe to approach the caged-off VIP seating. Pauly watched them slide through the crowd, took one step from his post as they emerged and extended a gnarled right hand. Joe nodded as Nick took the preferred paw and watched a small green dot slide up and down the wide arm. While hand signs prove effective through a wall of sound, they don't work too well if you're looking the other way. This was a common problem until Griff showed up with a laser-sighted hand gun. Got Nick thinking and soon the small hand-held pointers were part of everyone's kit. Lanyard around the wrist and clasped in the fist the short turned alloyed tube also increased punching power considerably. A popular and useful tool.

Nick signed his friends and queried the dot. The two heads turned, eyes casting out across the auditorium and dropped to the floor below to spy John the Ewok frantically slapping the top of his head and waving at the now obscured front door.

Nick didn't hear Joe say "Ah shit" with his ears, he heard him with his stomach.

Joe took a full half second to weigh his options. As he waved Pauly 'come'! He caught the 'yes me too' in Nick's pivot. A quick grin twitched his lips as they slid back into the crowd to slither to the stairs.

While the doors behind Clive were all timber the outward opening side portals weren't nearly so robust. Four inch glass squares set in a lattice of wood. Swung closed when the garden erupted, they exploded inward with a shower of shards and splinters as the three broke through from the fast fleeing crush.

Six in the crew with Nick and his crew plus Robbie made ten. Nick stepped tho the right and peered through the obscured glass panels, obscured by a broad back and shoulders six feet from the ground. Fists and feet flying like fury. The dozen pub bouncers were divided in teams of two, big Tony and his Tongan mate Marley, the best of 'em. The ones that would not run.

"That's BT in the corner and Marley's at the bottom step. I'll go right and ambush the arseholes and Tony, you guys go straight out and left, drag Marley back to the top step. We'll meet you there, make the bastards fight uphill. Don't get dragged down the steps. Go."

Ten bodies hit the centre of the double doors in a wedge. As the right flew opened, it glanced an elbow, part of an arm, part of a hand, part of sharpened 12-inch screw driver arcing towards Tony exposed kidney. Nick cut down with his left forearm and continued the circle. As the knife man's right forearm crashed into his neck and shoulder Nick reached up and grabbed his left wrist, jerked down and bent his knees, then drove the right one back up to snap the floating rib just as the now twisted elbow separated.

Tony's eyes met Nick's, said "Thanks a lot, your back's covered for rest of this lifetime."

Broken ribs went sideways, took two of his mates across the porch and down the steps, Nick and Tony surged after and stopped at the top. A good line, made of good people. Shoulder to shoulder, fists and feet flying, winkle picker punching holes, big fists breaking faces, elbows and knees for those coming closer, head butt and eye gauge for those way too close. A furious battle for all of five minutes, no one can sprint for six. John the Ewok took one and went down as a tricked up Ford truck cruised past, the red headed driver took stock. One hundred yards south and into his U-turn as Louis' conversational tone reached Nick's blood drumming ears.

"Tough bastards heh? Half of 'em keep getting up."

Nick weaved past a left and under a right, came up with a slap kick to the nuts and a hard left hook to the now open jaw. As the hinges snapped he reported across his shoulder.

"That one won't, you in or what?"

"Got Rikki on?"

"Yeah?"

The fat right hand that dove into the back of Nick's jeans emerged with a thirty inch close linked steel chain, a half kilo of tear dropped shaped steel on each end. Folded in half, a great weapon when not amongst friends.

When the fight erupted the bike guards had run to the brawl, a tonne and half of Ford ignored til it crashed through twenty long front forks. Three steps up and facing the road the defender saw it unfold, for back turned attackers a shocking surprise, distraction enough for a dozen clean shots and a flying fat greek through the line, manriki propeller in front. The tide had begun to turn. At the back of the pack helmets emerged as they regrouped to charge again. One in the driveway took a bullbar to the spine as the Ford came into the fray. Meat cleaver in his right, long carver in his left, the manic driver emerged. Choppers at the back, madness in the middle and a strong line now stepping forward; like

Bondi cockroaches in a fresh-lit kitchen, blood spatted colours fled to the dark.

Pub bouncers appeared, timed to a tee. The furious brawl descended to washing up.

As sirens approached, Nick gathered his crew.

Mark tried to turn back to his truck.

"Can't be here when the cops arrive, they'll fuck me up."

"It's ok, chill, that's ambulances from the hospital. Cops won't be here for an hour. Too many fighters, they'll call cars from a dozen suburbs before they come down."

Nick took two minutes to set his troops.

"Bill, you're with Mark and Robbie, get to Brian's, tell him what's up then get down to Heather's, stay out of sight until the rest of us get there. Blues'll be there somewhere discrete."

"Where are you and Dave?"

"We got one more stopover, Bondi, won't be long. Louis, you coming or what?"

"Fuck that. I got bumps and chunks out of my head from that chain thing and that little blond bar maid's real keen to play nurse. I'm staying here mate."

"Smart call son, good luck. Hey, thanks."

The team split, three and two.

BONDI

WITH ALL THE EXCITEMENT out the front, and sirens coming closer, by the time they reached the truck there was only one thief working the car park.

Nick said "Boo" and the door breaker spun and sprinted into Dave's chest, who promptly jumped up and down on the unhappy teen's knees and elbows. While Nick dragged their new acquaintance to a spot less public, Dave started the car. Out the driveway and South on Arden, up the hill and down to Bronte, skirt the coast and glamarama.

One beach from Bondi the U-shaped bay was nicknamed for its weekday popularity with gambler's wives. Too many young girls coming up, shaking fresh meat at cashed-up husbands, must keep the legs, abs and tan. A half hour a day on a surf board or ski keeps a girl trim, taught and terrific, makes the beach look good too. Popular little spot, Tamarama.

With wheels in motion and a few minute's grace, Nick allowed himself to relax. Heedless of voice security, Dave took the moment. "Finally, alone. You had something you wanted to tell me, and what's with all the introductions?"

"Hardly alone." Nick glanced at armrests and pictured Angie straining at the earphones.

A major part of his plan required Tony's input. Might as well give him something to start thinking about.

"All good people to know mate. Staunch. You stand for them and they'll kill or die for you, every one of them every time. Hard out here on your own. The way the town's going, you stay in this world much longer and you're going to need them. Every one of them's different, even the brothers. They'll give you good information, and watch your back. Half of them live in the straight world too. They're going to get more important."

"What's that shit. You've got my back and I'm happy with that. News from the straight world? Who cares? Can't trust those fuckers. You showed me yourself. There's no penalties for deceit. Right from the top. Politicians got it written in their rules. Say whatever they want on their club house floor, truth, gossip, fiction or flat out lies, no penalty. Money jugglers, strip a company, bad luck, bankrupt. Have to retire to the wife's spare mansion out Vaucluse way. Get behind the big iron gate and count my ten or twenty million payout. Forklift driver from the factory floor can get on the end of the dole queue. No penalty. How about their business ethics? Matter of fact, would you leave your ten-year-old son with a priest? Thanks mate, but I'd rather listen to people who live by the rules."

"You've seen what the McCoys will do, you reckon they don't live by the rules?"

"Oh yeah, but they're not square heads."

"They both got steady straight jobs mate. Bloody good ones too. Just what I'm saying. The towns going too grey.

Not so long ago it was cops, crooks and the competition, had to have a damn good reason to shoot you. Now every fuckwit with an attitude's carrying a gun."

"Thought you said people don't change."

"It's not the people, no, they don't change, it's the town. It's like rats in a box. When there is four of 'em they'll eat the best bits, sleep long and lazy and fuck slow and often. All good. When there's forty of them they'll eat the paint off the walls, sleep with teeth bared and one eye open and fight to the death over four fifths of fuck all. Town's getting crowded mate, I've had enough of it."

"Come on, it's not that bad. Most of these guys are sheep, they won't be carrying, coupla blades maybe, but so what? Okay there's a couple of Tony's guys or Frankie's but they'd have to be insane to pull a trigger outside Heather's, you reckon that wouldn't cause a shit storm."

"Don't be surprised son. That'd serve 'em real well. Chaos, throws all the pieces up in the air, knock the opposition and sweep it all up once the dust settles. Just politics, predictable. A pain in the arse, but predictable. No, tonight's not the problem."

"So, what is? Got anything to do with you disappearing from us?"

"Yeah mate it does."

They rounded the north end of the beach still aways to their next stop. Nick figured it was time and Angie should get a laugh out of the first half.

"Tell you a story. Remember the night we ran over the Porsche? That new black thing double parked outside the ice cream shop under Les Girls. Round the corner, up over the back of it and kept going? Well, turns out it belongs to some white collar thief out Vaucluse way. Robby something or other his name came out in the paper for shooting a burglar. Anyway he's robbed more people than any of his mates that quarter so he's bought himself a nice shiny new penis extension. He's had some leggie receptionist out slumming, showing what a hero he was. Fucked the car, put some dents in his ego too. Anyway he's got a quid so he splashed some about and found out I was driving. So he's fronted Brian's and demanded some ridiculous amount of money, now Brian knows never to trust anyone wearing a tie so Charlie give him a slap and threw him out.

Prick's not satisfied and not real smart either. You've met Jim haven't you? Big blond bloke, blue eyes big teeth, lives up on Ben Buckler point, comes over the house for sparring and choke holds. Makes his money driving bookies to the races. This Rodney prick, he's part of race crowd, big bettor, he's asked around and got hold of Jim. Offered him a shit load of money to put a hit on me, still doesn't know what I look like. Funny as. Jim's organised a meeting, told him the hitter will be there so bring the cash. We've sat down for about twenty minutes and listened to this soft cock, and then Jim's told him my name. Funniest fucking thing you ever saw. He's literally shit himself, threw the money up in the air and out the door he went at about two hundred miles an hour, and stank. Couldn't chase him, we're both rolling around the floor laughing, wouldn't want to touch him anyway. Persistent prick though."

Into Campbell Parade and down the hill, Nick went quiet as they cruised past the Lamrock Café. A favoured breakfast nook for tourists and locals alike. Considering the number of attractive professional women who chose to frequent the Lamrock, it was one of Nick's as well. Nick, he soured at the memory.

Susie was a pretty girl. Smart, good family, well educated. Had a mostly successful boutique just down from the café, bit of bad luck about the two hundred dollar a day heroin habit. She kept her act well together but heroin is an expensive hobby and hard to hide in business accounts. When Robby's men found her, with a gram and half of pure, a head and shoulders photo of Nick and the key to Robby's beachside apartment, she grudgingly accepted his deal.

"Just fuck him to sleep and we'll do the rest."

The soft sound of 'sorry Nick,' something in the tone. He cracked his eyelids to a harsh and blinding glare. Left hand questing he found tender skin and a silken slip, moving, away, quickly, a tremble in the flesh.

His right hand grabbed a hunk of pillow and dragged it across his head and shoulders as the first strike slammed down. That hurt, would leave a welt as well. Nick was as old school as pennies and pounds. From time to time punishments were sometimes necessary, but always face to face and always with a conversation.

Style did matter.

To take a baseball bat to a seemingly sleeping victim was not on.

The second and third strikes proved even less successful as the now furious enforcer flipped sides, closed and grasped for silent assailant, still all unaware of the room's other occupant, a now terrified swindler with a cute little 32. Up until now the night had been going all his way.

Nick had been hit before, more than once. The angle of the blows told him where to search. Left arm fired upwards between the batsman's legs and took him in the ice cream hold, "Would you like crushed nuts with that sir?" Pain.

As Mr Baseball curled into a C and dropped a knee on the bed in support, Nick's right palm caught him by the throat and closed fingers to crush both carotid arteries shut. Using his left elbow to pivot he rolled right to hurl the now body weight helpful attacker towards a vaguely remembered window. Tucked legs heaving, he thrust. Rodney stood shocked, still in the way. As the hired thug's forehead crashed into his teeth he threw up his hands in reactive defence, the right index finger clenched around a trigger. A sudden small hole appeared between Babe Ruth's shoulder and neck. A deep one, but little blood, it went down through the heart and stopped it, collapsed one lung and then embedded in the hip. No exit wound, and very neat. Made him very dead.

The Porsche bedevilled money juggler lived a long hard second in contemplation of a murder charge before the glass cracked behind and all his worries were over.

Thirty feet backwards real quick.

The glass in his arse and weight on his chest too fast to be felt, before a spike-topped cast iron fence ended his problems with the Department of Taxation.

New problems for Nick just begun.

Time to put his pants on.

Too much noise.

That would be the screaming boutique owner cringing by the bedside.

A quick calculation. Knock her out or take the time to calm her down?

Better if she stays on her feet.

One hand gently across her wide mouth, eyes and lips telling the same story, "Panic bad, calm good."

In the world of smack addicts, Susie may well have stood a cut above, but the instincts remained the same. Faced with disaster any junkie's reflex snaps to self-centred survival. Nick showed her a small light at the end of the dark tunnel, a chance. Her attention drawing vocals quietened.

"Listen girl! You got us into this, now you gotta help us get out. Find clean linen, sheets and pillow slips, make the bed and meet me at the back door."

Like most Bondi apartment blocks, the back door from the kitchen opened to and exposed a rear stairwell with a chute-served incinerator chimney stack.

Nick bundled the bedding, wiped out the ashtray to collect the roach from the joint they shared, smashed the champagne bottle into the linen and jammed the lot down the chute. With one end alight and followed by a blazing newspaper it soon became the best kind of evidence. Gone.

Back inside to check the girl, now doing good, clean the glasses and put them back just like they'd never been used.

Out the back door and gone just as the sirens pulled up in front.

Susie took a day off work.

Nick took a plane to Cairns.

"Persistent?" Dave queried.

"Yeah, he did try to hire another bloke, some idiot with a bat."

"What happened there?"

"Seems they had a bit of a falling out, haven't heard from him since."

"Reckon he'll be back?"

"Can't see it. I'd say he got the point after his last mistake."

Dave's memory clicked. Headline television news, a full page in the Sydney Telegraph. 'Burglar meets banker. A dead heat.' Just about the time Nick disappeared.

He made the effort to lighten Nick's darkening mood.

"Good then, pricks gone, no worries. That's the problem with you cranky old fucks, you live too much in the past. We're here, now, having fun."

He paused.

"Which reminds me. Just why are we here now?"

KEVIN

WHILE NICK WAS WELL aware of his auditory audience, and liked to play his cards close to his chest, Angel had been a mate for a lifetime. The canny and ultimately connected dago was anything but a threat. For the first time in his life Nick felt ok, even comfortable, about being overheard. If Tony wanted him at Darling Point for breakfast Angelo would do what he could to keep him alive at least that long. Comfort, a small one maybe but definitely a comfort. He answered Dave's query out loud.

"Just reminded myself of Jim. If he's home he would be handy to bring along," then thought to himself, if not, at least the conversation and time wasting should earn the blue eyed bastard some kudos with the old family, good tokens to carry in his line of work, I owe him that much at least.

Aloud again he added "go right here and up and around the Ben Buckler loop. If his lights are on I'll give him a call, if not, straight back to the Euro club. No lights showed at the dark humoured debt collector's cliffside eyrie, so back down the beachfront and up the short hill to the club.

A half century ago and a half a world, away the Euro had been the town square. The heart and the stage of the people.

Hot tea and gossip and matrons match making, sweet sticky buns and clouded pipes, vodka and laughter a'foot. Commercial agreements sealed with a handshake ensured a lifetime of trust, where sons and daughters joined in marriage gave great cause to dance.

Then came the dark days. The square's all destroyed, the people dispersed. A decade would pass before rediscovered kinfolk, in contact from a far southern land, offered hope. The town square rebuilt next to a beach.

Not open and airy and easy to pierce but four square and solid and five stories tall. An island of family-centred peace and fraternity in the surf-besotted sea of the Bondi community. As law abiding a community as any could wish, but far from naive. Memories live long in people with scars. Sons became doctors, nephews became lawyers, daughters and wives guarded kitchen and stock.

Yossi got an office upstairs.

He eyed the monitors lining one wall and watched the young men earning their pay. Sharp eyed and lithe with gentle wide smiles, quite good with hand guns as well. The white haired old dear, with teacake and a cane, chairs and obstructions all melted away as she crossed the floor to her table crowded with sisters and nieces.

A gentle pat on the shoulder, a seat taken and respectful conversation with a wise and old man sunk just a little too deep in reverie.

He was pleased with his boys.

The top centre screen showed a van slide to a stop right outside, the engine died and the lights blinked twice for hello. Not completely necessary but appreciated just the same. He pulled a pen from his pocket, slid a card across the desk and wrote an address on the back. A thin paper card and otherwise blank, he knew it would burn soon enough. He eased to his feet and wandered downstairs. Dave flicked the lights a second time and turned to his passenger. "We're wasting a lot of time Nick, Now why are we here? We got no time for visiting."

"Just needed a few minutes for the phone call."

"Why do you want to call?"

Nick sighed. "Not me mate, look, I need Lionel and I would sure like to have Kevin on side. They're still both working the game. So, do you know the venue this week? I don't".

"No."

"Yossi does."

Nick pointed to the armrest and continued.

"Considering how many people have an interest in the dance tonight, I bet ya he already knows we are on the way."

Through lessons learned hard, the club founders came to appropriately appreciate the value of information from, and occasional intervention by, the denizens of the dark side. A most useful income stream, foolish to be neglected as well. To prevent conversations over heard which may well disturb the matriarchal ambience, beloved black sheep uncles, cousins and brothers of the traditionally large families required alternate venue.

Visitations of uniformed authority were also to be actively avoided, the embarrassment severe, for some patrons the memories spurred unbearable. The need was perceived, the game was on.

At first a small group of elders, both puzzled new Australians and those who made the long journeys generations before, gathered on a leafy back porch to push dominos and cards around a green top table. They played for match sticks and half pennies and discussed the ways a shattered and bewildered group may make its future in this world. The mistress of the house provided tea and snacks, a pile of small change left on the table for recompense.

Ideas were touted, advisers invited, and some of the match sticks and halfpennies grew to shillings and pounds. When pounds turned to dollars and pennies to cents the pile on the table turned to a mound. While invitation only, success breads expansion and so the list grew. Four tables now and the need for more space demands the rental of public rooms. Well perhaps semi period. Small jealousies developed, as they do when the mound becomes many, so the game became mobile, no one to claim owner or to be labelled as such when visited by gaming squad officers somehow left out of the loop. Taxes were paid of course, of a sort. While sons grew tall and strong, to maintain the required privacy to recognise and defuse simmering disputes, outsiders were needed, disconnected, unbiased, close mouthed and capable. Kevin and Lionel.

While as dangerous as many, and more so than most, their regular well-paid gig, with the occasional extravagant bonus left them unknown to the mainstream of thuggery. Just what Nick needed.

As far spaced as possible, both left and right, from the bright light façade, to purpose built doors. Narrow, no handles, discernible only by the fine crack between their solid timber construction and the surrounding masonry. Silent to open and quickly to close, they allowed athletic young men to emerge. They sauntered quite casually to the foot of the stairs, in line with an unfamiliar tan van now occupying the normally sacrosanct cab rank. No one had emerged, suspicious in itself. As they approached the unknown visitor Dave began to bristle, Nick began to smile, he offered a small cryptic aside.

"You know what Dave? Taxis are good."

His answer was attention shifting "what?" from the bewildered driver.

More awkward questions were averted as the front doors slid open and a grinning Yossi skipped lightly down the steps.

He patted the young men, one broad shoulder each.

"Good. See me inside."

Their vigilance and response would be noted and the nightly debrief.

Smooth and almost synchronised, the boys turned indoors, Yossi stepped forward and the kerbside window rolled down.

"G'day mate," as he offered a hand shake with something white in his palm.

Nick's hand came away, the message received.

He scanned it once and turned it over, turned it back and read it again, once more to be sure as he applied the flam.

Yossi noted the triple take and joked.

"Early dementia, that memory loss, too many shots to the head old fella."

"Measure twice, cut once old son. I've knocked on the wrong door before. Some mistakes I try not to repeat, and you should know more about being polite to your elders."

Good friends by now, the banter was easy.

"No need to knock, they will be waiting."

Nick was surprised by the comment.

"Early finish."

"Young fella up your way has not made himself any friends. The boys running the game are happy to let them go where they will do the most good. No one's complaining."

"Jesus Yos, who else knows about this?"

"Don't worry mate, like I said, no friends, just people he pays. No one will utter a word."

He added a nod to the driver.

"You been good?"

"Yes sir."

Two words only. The tone steeped in respect. Nick heard it and hid his smile, pleased with his sidekick's growing good sense.

"Good seeing ya mate, gotta go."

Yossi turned back inside to close the club, happy to be able to help. They started the car and asked.

"Where to?"

"Blair Street, mate. Saint Ann's school hall."

"Bullshit. Gambling in a church?"

"Easy mate. All in the terminology, they pay top dollar too. Call it Russian bingo and the catholics trip over themselves collecting the rent."

A short hop from the Euro, Dave was soon wheeling in the narrow street behind the school. He turned into the driveway, the headlights sweeping a living statue. A rich black mane exploded from its forehead and swept back to the shoulders, wide and thick and end-caped with the arms of a silverback.

So long since his surname had been spoken, it was a thing forgotten so, like emperors of old, he used just the one appellation.

Nick tapped Dave on the shoulder.

"Say hello to Lionel."

Some said his absent father was a Frenchman, so arrogant not a trace of his Maori mother appeared. A dedicated alcoholic, she soon lost him to the state welfare system. A small, weak white boy in a Polynesian orphanage, he might have expected hell, but he was lucky.

Rarotongan's, Tongans and Samoans, Fijians, Tahitians and Maori, even a couple of brothers from far off Hawaii. Sensible people, they knew a cover of white skin meant nothing and continued to hate everyone with equal enthusiasm.

Dave lowered his window and offered his hand. Lionel bent at his waist and peered across the front seat to spot Nick. He knew the van, had ridden in it often enough but liked to make sure before he surrendered his right, even if only for an up and down pump.

"G'day."

With Gallic pride stamped into his mitochondria, taking a step backwards was just about the only thing he couldn't do.

At 75 kilograms he sampled all the South Pacific had to offer. Boxing, kungfu and karate, he punched holes in anyone silly enough to stand in front of him. Stand six inches from your face and kick you hard in the back of the head, not a problem.

With non-judicious use of black market steroids he ballooned to 110.

Couldn't fuck too well. But by god he could fight.

"Ready!" he thought.

An anonymous fishing boat to Tasmania, jump ship with a mate, half's in a Datsun 120Y, he wound his way up the coast to Bondi. Within two days he had discovered the glitter strip. A handsome man, with no regard to the value of money, the dancing girls were pleased with his arrival. Three months off the steroid needle and erectile dysfunction already forgotten, he was happy too. With no education or qualification and preferring to work where he played, like many before the wandering Kiwi sought door work on

Darlinghurst Road.

At first ignored and later refused, his reasoning followed a familiar pattern.

"Knock out the guys out the front and the bosses inside got no choice."

It was a strategy that worked quite a treat in South Auckland, successful as well in the Cross.

Three months on the job and aside from the non-taxable fringe benefits, he knew he didn't fit. He couldn't bring himself to punch one more drunken punter who had the temerity to complain about ten dollar beers.

Just too damn nice a bloke.

By this time he had heard of Nick, even seen him perform on a couple of notable occasions.

Spent a month in Brian's, sipping lemonade.

He was noticed, and noted, and questions were asked.

"Not a cop?"

"No, no, just a bloody good bloke, especially for a Kiwi, can fight a bit too. Tough fucker as well, and the girlies like him."

Nick met him, they shook.

"Don't worry son, I'll find you a nook."

Dave released the hand and Lionel stayed bent at the hip to keep his eyes on Nick as he queried the Kiwi.

"Where's Kev?"

"He's inside getting the pays."

Though tighter with a quid than his partner, Kev was a true country gent with a smile as wide as the morning sun.

As Aussie as Akubra he was born to the dry cattle lands of mid N.S.W. By the age of 15 he already had his fill of toil tackling wild bush cattle and breaking mad brumbies, somehow he just knew there had to be better things to look at each day than a fly-crusted rear end of the startled steer. It had been a full year since the town publican had given him the nod, now at 6ft 2 and fifteen stone he could hold his beer with the best. The local coppers knew him of course but common sense prevails in the bush, he'd earned his drink and no one complained when they turned a blind eye to the over grown boy at the bar.

In his longest speech yet, in the concrete slab "beer garden," through red grit-ground vocal cords, one Saturday night he laid out his plans to his mates.

"Wanna see some things, have some fun."

Come Sunday he hitched a ride on the beef truck and headed for the bright lights of Penrith. He hadn't considered when he might be coming home, good thing, avoided a lot of disappointment that way.

Good bloke Kev, the town came to miss him that much they eventually built a zoo out that way. Filled it full of wild African rhinos just to remember him by.

Ten years flew past before he met Nick, he put on some weight, seen some things and had some fun, got a job as a truck driver too, didn't like it much. In the days before driving home drunk became a social taboo, the highways and byways were lined with empty V.B. cans. Travel times between country towns were measured in 6 packs.

If you wanted a thousand punters in the pub you needed a big car park. Enough room in fact for 100

Holden's, 90 Fords, 6 trucks and a couple of Toyotas. A bit of space over in the corner for blow-ins as well, that's where Lionel had parked the love of his life. As soon as he saw her, the Datsun was gone. A blown G.T.O. with buckets of power, trimmed in true South Auckland style, purple paint and fat silver wheels and a couple of dice hung from the rear view mirror. He named her Maybelline.

As rough as guts and as cool as a cucumber in winter time, a western suburbs band named Bandana had played the Coogee Bay two weeks before and Nick was wrapped in their hard driving rock 'n roll. He and Lionel had worked that night and had enjoyed the gig so much they had laid on a couple of dancing girls for the boys in the green room for the after party. Got themselves an invite to the next gig, a West Penrith pub on a Sunday afternoon. Way out west for a couple of city boys. Nick had a couple of days to spare and Lionel had his first chance to open up Maybelline on a wide fast road. They had made a day of it.

All damn good, until they shook the band's hands, "Thanks guys be seeing ya," and returned to their far corner parking spot.

The thing about West Penrith car parks, if you were a local thug, with brothers and cousins patched into an outlaw gang, with an eye for fat silver wheels and a habit of not paying for them, far corner parking spots were a good place to shop. These five guys were organised, even had a 2-tonne trolley jack in the back of one of their ratty utes. They had it under Maybelline's nose and had just started to pump the handle when the two happy strangers strolled around the nose of a Mac prime mover that had limited their view until just that moment.

You could tell Lionel got angry from the bright red face and the steam out of his ears. Nick would later swear he even saw flames shoot out of his arse as he rocketed into the guy with his hand on the handle. Handle guy saw none of it but his mates in the ward filled him in three weeks later when he was brought out of the induced coma. The multiple skull fractures were starting to heal and in time might make a full recovery. Nick started on the other four, he knew Lionel would be over to help when he finished his entrée. They had done this kind of thing a couple of times before.

When fighting groups, Nick had a bit of a pattern. Smack number one in the groin with a slap kick, number two got a flail fingered slap in the eye, very fast, very painful, kind of "wait here I'll be back," number three caught a hard right hand to the point of the chin, out! A good referee would have stopped the fight and called for a doctor, guys in the fourth row would have heard the bones break.

Number four was quicker than most. Smashed a half full V.B. stubbie on the back of Nick's head before Lionel caught him. The shot drove a now angry Nick back to unlucky number two and enraged the big chested Kiwi even more. With a handful of ass and a good grip on a hank of hair, he hoisted the bloody fingered thief to shoulder height and slammed his head into the side of the Mac, twice. Just once more than necessary.

He woke the bloke sleeping in the back. A bloke named Kev. A bloke who sat up and winced at the still unfamiliar plaster cast scrapped across his hip, then pulled the curtain across the small sleeping cab window and peered out just in time to see Nick finish number two. Kev didn't know the two guys standing but recognised the four lying down as part of a group of ten whose behaviour he had objected to two weeks before. He'd been doing well until an unseen shifting spanner had met his temple. Still alive simply because he was a tough fucker, Kev had woken in an ambulance with a cracked skull, a broken arm and bruises all over where they had tap danced up and down. He convinced the attending physician to include two thin inch wide steel straps in the plaster and kept parking behind the pub in the hope of catching them one or two at a time. Seeing Lionel and Nick he had woken up happy. Some people call it karma.

Nick put his hand to the back of his head, it came away bloody. Just a bit disappointed at his lack of vision and a little bit peeved at Lionel's lack of alacrity, he was about to offer a comment when the rumbling sound intruded.

The dozen patched members had just finished a run up the mountain to Katoomba and rolled in to their local to have a beer with their brothers. The road boss blinked twice and blinked twice when he spotted the boys all laid out in pools of blood with two strangers standing over them. Hot engine bikes growled to a halt and side stands crashed down as the foul tempered outlaws dismounted.

High in his unseen eyrie, the vengeance-starved trucker watched it unfold.

Now, bush-educated Kev couldn't spell "hesitate" to save his life. Wouldn't know what it meant anyway. He knew these pricks, painfully. The small waking smirk snapped into a huge dawning grin. Last time they had met it had been ten to one and he almost got away with it, this time it was twelve to three. And these boys looked the goods. This time it would be different.

A big gnarled paw wrapped around the in-cab fire extinguisher while a heavy cab door kicked open took the nearest road-glazed rider square in the face. Kev gave them all his best impression of an angry scrub bull roar as he leapt onto the near end of the arc. Surprised the fuck out of everyone. One head hit the ground, hard, eleven others swivelled to spot this loud intrusion. Two heads held focus. They took the unexpected but very welcome distraction to launch their own attacks. Kicks, punches, elbows and head butts, no rules. Damp fingers pushed the eyes back and a hook on top of the suborbital bone slackens the knees, drives the slack-jawed screaming head down onto a hard rising knee of your own.

Devastating.

A small red fire extinguisher grown slick and more scarlet with fresh blood, discarded to make way for more satisfying knuckle on bone.

Soon there was one. A broad-shouldered, beer-gutted full bearded behemoth.

Lionel grabbed his right wrist and pulled as Kev grabbed the left and tried to claim him. They crossed eyes and yanked. To Nick, bereft of opponents and with a moment to reflect, it looked nothing so much as two angry seagulls fighting over the last picnic chip.

Cracked him up. Fell over laughing, bleeding but laughing. The two new-found brothers, kindred souls, appreciated the humour. Took just a moment for Lionel's right fist to fracture the behemoth's head, must have weakened the structure as the face went concave behind a hard-driven plaster cast. They let the torso drop and bent together to help the smaller man to his feet.

"G'day, name's Kev. Pleased to meet ya." Ever the country gent. Introductions made, the trio made time for a quick chat. After a brawl the cops were always slow to arrive. Usually about twenty minutes behind the last ambulance. Turned out Kev had had enough of his trucking career. Had only kept the Mac driving gig in the hope of catching those bastards on the highway.

"Ever done any bouncing? Protection work?" from Nick.

"No, don't know if I would be any good at it."

Nick knew, Lionel was sure.

Never one for a lot of possessions it turned out just about everything Kev owned was in the back of the Mac. Took about five minutes to transfer his swag to the back of Maybelline. Keys behind the visor and a goodbye note.

"Trev will know where to find the truck."

No explanation as to who Trev might be.

The boys headed east. Two going home, one to a whole new set of "see some things, have some fun".

What with Maybelline's throaty purr reverberating through the thick seats, Bandanas' demo tape rocking from the speakers, and the healthy-shared booty from a pile of embossed leather wallets and billfolds, "always good to keep ID's and addresses", not to mention a thick pile of notes, they were already having fun. A brand new band of brothers, already as tight as a fish's asshole.

BETTER DAYS

A FIRE DOOR AT the school hall rear cracked open, the bright-lit rectangle filled for a moment with a smooth moving shadow. It slid down the short flight of stone steps to the dark side of the van.

"G'day mate," as a right hand was offered through the passenger window.

From the timbre of the voice Dave was not surprised to see Nick's hand disappear into the enveloping meat.

Handshake exchanged, Nick used his thumb to point to the driver.

"Dave."

Then his index finger to introduce the shadow.

"Kev."

"G'day."

Dave's reply was lost as two voices in unison declared "Time to go."

A pique of jealousy flowed through his chest, not seen each other for months, yet mind and intent fell into lockstep in a heartbeat. He sensed the deep waters between Nick and the Kiwi and the shallowness of his own emotion, encouraged it to drift away. Nick felt the wave, smiled inside and thought, 'he's getting better, good, about time, too'. Never one to waste words, Kev welcomed the interruption. He'd heard about Nick's new mate. Trusted by all who came to know him and particularly by Yossi, he'd soon come to discover their arrangement.

He might talk to the boy later. Once he got to know him a bit.

Depending on how he behaved in tonight's situation.

Grown a touch judgemental had Kev, since his move to town. Clever bloke, the city can teach you that, if you pay attention. The springs shrank as the two new players climbed in the back. Lionel knew the Porsche driver's story. In an early morning drinking session he, Charlie and Jim had shared a good laugh about it. Nick's lack of nightclub pallor which, night or day, shone like a beacon to those who knew him, combined with his immediate disappearance following the money juggler's well-reported freefall accident resisting a burglary … were just too coincidental.

Especially since the burglar apparently used a baseball bat to pick the lock. He also enjoyed the breakfast at the Lamrock. He'd noted a sweet young thing down there, not far from the reported fatal fall, who'd given Nick the 'once over' more than once. She'd also seemed to become conspicuous in her absence just about that time. Like any good scallywag he'd easily identified the discreet heroin dealer with whom she fairly regularly exchanged a chat. On her re-emergence he no longer seemed to be a member of her social set. There was a story there, he was sure of it. An inquisitive bastard by nature and always up for a challenge, he wondered whether he might be able to pry some of it from his close-mouthed mate.

Once Dave had backed from the driveway and negotiated the few lefts and rights that led to Blair Street, Bellevue Hill, and their eventual destination in the Cross, he dropped his question, knowing Nick, he made it an oblique one and hoped it would lead in the direction that he wanted.

"Well, Mr Dissappearo, show up all sun tanned out of the blue, haven't heard from you for a while. Thought you were dead. What you been up to? Hiding out from that ferocious Robbie Adden?"

He should have known better, Nick was born suspicious, the nature of his profession occasionally required surprise travel. His return often met with a silent nod and handshake, usually with an envelope full of fifties. When questions were asked, they were always precise and always to do with whether the previous owner of the fifties had spent his money wisely.

While the front of his mind cobbled together the action plan he'd set his subconscious to play with the factors involved in his future, he felt no threat in his friend's query. Probably just curiosity. That was one of his mate's two minor bad habits. Like the other, which did involve opiates and dancing girls, not a danger unless overly indulged.

Still, it had nothing to do with tonight's events, so he threw it in with the subconscious mix. Needed a moment for the bubbles to arrive so he threw "just a sec" over his shoulder and prodded Dave on the bicep.

"One more quick stop, at the cab rank."

"What??? What for? How long is that going to take?"

"Not long, just need a coupla taxis." He let the direction turn their attention while he quietly lined up his own thoughts. He quietly listed them.

1. Getting time to retire.
2. There's no pension plan in the punching profession.
3. Tone's got plenty, and he owes me a big one.
4. Breakfast will be important. It was a surprise request but it shouldn't have been. The old man's got ears everywhere, he glanced at the armrest to lock in that thought.
5. Bill's invited. No, not invited, more like required.
6. Lionel's there, too.
7. He's a devious old bastard and sure to have plans of his own.
8. Looks like they include me.
9. Be good to throw a token or two of my own onto his table.
10. Lionel wants a story.

He turned his head to the back of the van, and saw Lionel's ears perk up. He was certain the other end of the armrest, or wherever the mike was planted, was doing the same. "Who, that prick in the Porsche, no mate, forgotten all about him. No, I been exploring, bloody good trip too, found paradise in the sun."

Kev offered a comment, rare, but dry and wry as usual. "Oh yeah, and whose stupid enough to name their daughter Paradise when you are in town?"

That got a bark of laughter from two of his mates and a happy protestation from Nick. "Hey, pull up you horny bastard, it's not all about sex, true, there was a girl involved, a cutie too, but she wasn't the best part."

"Ok, so where'd you go?"

"Well, Cairns first, but the good stuff didn't start till I got to Yorkie's Knob."

"What the fuck! You gone queer, and who the fuck's Yorkie?"

"Not a bloke, you dill, a place, a peninsular about twenty clicks north of Cairns with a rock at the end of it, a big hill actually. Somehow it got the name Yorkie's Knob."

"Never heard of the joint, how'd you end up there?"

"Shut up and I'll tell ya, anyway, got out of the shower one afternoon and saw myself in the mirror. Nearly blinded by the white. Thought, shit! haven't seen the sun for about a year, had about twelve grand from that juiced-up hay burner Al gave us the tip on, running at the Randwick Carnival so I thought "fuck, I'll duck up to Cairns for a coupla weeks. Get some vitamin D, might cheer me up a bit too, I'd been feeling a little tense". Lionel laughed. Nick gave him the "WHAT" look, and moved on. "Got out at the airport and there's these high ridges just to the west with walking tracks over them. Hadn't been there before, so ok, I'll get up there and have a look around, get the lie of the land, like. There's two tracks up there with real imaginative names. One's called Blue and the other one Red, ok, I'm a winner, I'll take the blue. Feeling all cocky. Got up to the top of the ridge, walking along, track's about two feet wide. Can see the city just to the south. Big port there, big bright buildings all over the place, even building a casino there.

Fuck that, had enough of that shit for a while. Just north a bit looks great, clean blue sea, couple of sailing boats tacking in and out and what looks like a hill sticking up out of the ocean, all covered in trees with just a couple roofs peeking through. Yeah, that's more like it. Post card stuff.

Walking along a bit further and just below me on the hillside there's this walking bush staying level with me. What the fuck? Brown hairy looking thing, about a metre across. I've stopped to look a bit closer and it stuck its head up. Not a bush, it's a thing called a cassowary. Ancient thing, dinosaur with feathers. I've looked at it, it's looked at me, and straight away breaks into a sprint, quick as. Run a diagonal up onto the track about twenty metres in front of him. Standing straight up, this thing's about seven foot tall. Ever seen a cranky rooster?. All puffed up with attitude and like, scatty, nervous body posture? Mindless-looking thing but you can just feel the anger pouring out of it. Great big three-toed claws on it, about a foot long, big bone spur, sticking out the back. Charges straight at me. Oh yeah. There's this bit of dead tree branch just off the side, I'll bat this cranky fucker, grabbed it up and its gone to powder in my hand. Dry as dust. I've shit myself, just off the track and slid a dozen metres down the hill. Grabbed a sapling to stop myself. Fucking thing's followed me. Saplings about two or three inches wide, flexible and springy, about three metres tall with a big green bushy head on it. I'm on one side of it, cassowary's on the other. I'm shaking this thing, moving from side to side and the bird's swapping its head from side to side too, trying to line me up. I'm looking at the claws on it, great fucking talons, rip your guts out no problem. Now I'm starting to get pissed off. I can see the newsprint in the telegraph "Nick Fallon Dead! Killed by giant chook!" Just too fucking embarrassing man. I start screaming and shouting, throwing handfuls of dirt and stones in its face.

Every time I move the tree, the head on it shakes and the bird backs up a couple of steps and looks up at its crown. I've got it confused. Anyway, thing keeps me bailed up for about ten minutes, terrified, then just backs off and saunters back up the track. I'm gone. Hundred miles an hour straight down the hill. Run, jump, slide, slip, drop, trees and bushes and shit, out of there!.

There's a suburb right at the bottom, Edge Hill, a good name, a cab rank, too. You little beauty! Take me where the sailing boats are, there's shit up there in them hills that will kill ya." Cab driver's all "look at you, shirt and back pack all scratched up, shit all over your jeans. What's the story?"

I did look like shit, so I've told him, he's all blasé "yeah, yeah those things will kill you alright, ripped the guts out of a tourist just a coupla months back."

"Why don't the city council get rid of it? That thing up there's like leaving a crocodile in a swimming pool."

"Can't do that mate, they're protected." "Protected? Give me a .38 and I'll give you protected. I'll give you roast fucking dinosaur." "Weird bugger, didn't get my attitude at all. Did show me where I could get a drink though. Told him the hill I'd spotted out of town, took me straight to the bottom of it. Yorkie's Knob Sailing Club. Terrific little place, just absolute basic. They got a couple of dozen big timber posts sticking up out on the water behind a breakwater wall. Handful of fishing boats tied to them but mostly sailing boats. Lots of multi-hulls, catamarans and trimarans. Perfect boats for the reefs up there. Club's just three demountables with a roof over them and a concrete slab in the middle.

Anyway there's this girl, owns one of the trimarans trading barramundi and mud crabs for coffee, Jack Daniels and fishing gear. She's the only other person drinking Jack and a bit better looking that the local blokes, so we got to talking. Barmaid at a pub, a bit further up the coast at Port Douglas. Got this neat little boat and days off gets away from the drunks and local shitheads just drifting up and down the reef. She's living on a shoestring and I've got nowhere to stay so I've done her a deal. Got the bits and pieces from the chandlers she wanted for the boat, a couple more bottles of Jack and some fins and diving stuff. She's offered me a couple of days down to Fitzroy Island, that's just off Cairns and back up to Port Douglas. Best deal I've done in twenty years. Brilliant. Couple of hours later we are down off Fitzroy, snorkelling about, looking at the reef and this school of fish comes up over a ledge and scares the hell out me. Maori wrasse. Huge things, giant heads on them, mouths about a foot across. Heaps of them. I've thought, oh great, first a giant angry chook and now these things are going to eat me, welcome to Queensland. She's grabbed my hand and signalled me, no, no, they are cool.

Amazing.

They're all around us, about six inches away. Come in, have a look and just drift along with you for a bit then another would come, taking turns. You can just about talk to them. Beautiful shit. Went on for about half an hour. Then they've had enough of us, and pissed off. Just phht and their gone.

Magic!

Anyway, a bit later were back on the boat and she's cooked up some of the best seafood you've ever eaten in your life. Red emperor for me, coral trout for her, and these little crayfish for an appetiser. Coupla drinks and a joint, and were parked up for the night.

More magic.

No lights anywhere, hardly any moon and a sky just brilliant with stars. So close you can feel yourself breathing in. You swell up five foot just sitting there."

Never one to miss a chance to be cheeky, Lionel chimed in. "Five foot? You'd reckon you'd stay there. Stop being a short arse."

Instead of the bristled retort he'd expected, he received a more measured reply "the thought did occur to me old son".

No one else in the car liked the sound of that.

"Next morning up anchor and off to Port. 'Bout half way there she's given me the tiller -- that's the steering wheel for you non-nautical types, gone down in the cabin, and come up with a couple of buckets of pilchards, bait fish that is for you street urchins. I'm thinking, shit lunch don't look too good, but no, not for eating, she starts feeding them over the side.

"What's this?"

"Dolphins."

"The ocean just explodes with them. Dozens of the fuckers. Trimaran, right? Three hulls. Straight away there's three of them in front of each hull, like outriders in front of a limo. There's others, heaps, leaping out of the water doing back-flips and shit. And all the time they are coming up to her, take a fish, give her like a nod, and fuck off. All real polite, one at a time, no pushing. Better people than people.

Girl's got tears in her eyes, that happy. I was about to bend her over the boom, express some appreciation like. Stopped me dead in my tracks. She did have it right. Sure beats the shit outta sitting at the bar debating damn dog shit with drunks on your day off.

I end up on the front centre prow. Dolphins stayed with us all the way to Port. Afternoon sun, dolphins dancing all over the joint, fucking glorious man."

Booked into the pub where she worked, The Central. You ever get up that way, it's worth a look, big beer garden, big meals, music all weekend and most of the week. Ran into Nick Barker doing a gig up there. Him and Nick Dreds doing a two-piece thing. Remember Dreds? He's living up there, had a couple of great nights with those guys. Remember Jimmy Blue eyes? He's up there too, got this tour business just out of town. A hammock, a light and an esky, nothing to it. You can sling the things just about anywhere. Took me up the Daintree a couple times, sleep on the beach and go wandering through the forest. Coconuts, mangoes and all kinds of tropical fruit all over the joint. Little stands of dope growing wild. All kinds of shellfish and barramundi jumping out of the water, air so clean it's a thousand-dollar detox just walking around. I could use some more of that shit."

He turned to face Lionel.

"Speaking of good food, we got a breakfast invitation at Tony's." There was no doubt which Tony he meant.

"Who?" from the surprised Kiwi.

"You, me and Bill."

"Bill the girl?"

"Yeah."

'What's that about?"

"Don't know, something to do with his grandson, find out more tomorrow."

While always lavish with his hospitality, Lionel knew the old man well enough to know an invitation to his table meant more than a meal. Between Nick's new-found love of all things outdoors, and the wily old manipulator's invitation to dine, the boys in the van were a touch nonplussed.

Gino, on the other hand, was having a whale of a time.

GINO

"WHAT A FUCKING NIGHT! How good is this?!" Happy as a pig in shit and with enough coke up his nose to topple the race card at the spring carnival, Gino was making plans. Predicting his future. Out loud, to anyone who cared to listen.

"Fuck cars!"

His past had been in the cut and shunt trade. Re-birthing stolen cars had become a lucrative business, especially the high end stuff. That many boys selling smack or flake out in the suburbs he could sell a Ferrari or a Lambo in a day. If that lazy mongrel crew he'd been saddled with would just get off their fat arses and find him that many cars. Good customers too. They were happy to pay in cash or product and didn't give a fuck where the cars came from. No insurance either, so when they broke one, as they often did, it was straight back to Gino's for another. Like selling homing pigeons. Tony had a string of workshops across the city. Out of the carpark or straight off the showroom floor from Ryde to Liverpool, he could disappear a newly stolen vehicle in less than ten minutes. Gino had started his working life as a panel beater before graduating to car thief. A fat one, greedy and savage. Not much older and looking for leverage in the first scam his father had trusted him to run, young Tony had found a soul mate.

Kindred spirits.

Despite rumoured misgivings from unnamed sources, his career had begun to rise. He was given a bat and a crew to run. Kids like himself, except for the fact that they enjoyed nothing more than the sound of police pursuit sirens, whilst he preferred to be tucked up safely miles away. Not someone who believed in leading from the front. He did understand the need to maintain appearances though. Little Tony had added debt collection to his duties so a growing, even if misplaced, reputation as a hard man was a necessary tool in trade.

Chaining some strung out debt-owing junkie to a chair, and he became quite scary, brave even. He and his bat had just the best time. Of course an audience was always necessary and always fools who couldn't tell cruelty from courage. Just like tonight, two new guys. Tony's idea.

"That stupid old prick won't hire anyone but Sicilians or Italians, mostly relatives, there's a shit load of wasted talent out there."

Gino's hiring skills.

"I know some mad fuckers, do anything for a dollar."

On contract from a little known, but growing crime family from the inner west, Mahmout and Fred were looking good. Dressed in Hugo Boss and paying close attention, Gino liked that in a lackey, made him look good. Ego food was his favourite meal.

Direct from Lebanon, their new lives purchased with the five kilos of smack taped to their bodies in a Beirut hotel room, and walked through Australian customs, these guys were familiar with war, keen even.

The boys from the soccer team may well be happy to throw a few kicks and punches, even pull a knife, but these guys liked guns. They'd brought their own, even supplied the overweight long-barrel .44 Gino presently enjoyed sliding in and out of the mouth of the naked, manacled girl set kneeling before his couch. A sadistic piece of shit.

Denise was having a bad enough night of her own, but still felt some sympathy for the friend and co-worker stretched the length of the couch beside him. Chosen for her tiny mouth and waist-length raven hair, Robin was having an evil night. Well practised and quite fond of kidnap and torture, Gino's recruits, had also brought a couple pairs of handcuffs on the off chance they could capture this Brian guy. Gino put them to use on his chosen pair. Ankles bound to the far end of the couch and manacled behind, he'd not removed the g-string she wore, had no intention of fucking her. Long hair tightly trapped under his left thigh, her face jammed down, anchored over his cock. Had another use for her tight little buttocks. From time to time he'd take the gun barrel from Denise's mouth and grate it against Robin's rear end. To emphasise points in his planning dissertation, he thrust the weapon high between the straining thighs, raised his thick calloused panel beater's hand high above his head and crash it down on her glowing cheeks. Made a stinging, incandescent arse and the head, with a mottled scream bouncing as far as the trapped mane would permit.

He liked emphasis.

Used it a lot.

And again.

"Fuck cars," as his hand slammed down, "this is the business". He growled at Heather. "Get me another drink, bitch, and add some love this time. Once that old prick is out of the way, you are mine. This whole fucking place is mine."

Heather stood stunned still for a second, what utter stupidity, saw Fred's ears twitch as well. While tonight's efforts were aimed at Brian, his 'old prick' reference could mean only one thing, a move on the old man. War like there hadn't been for a generation. Good God, these guys were dangerously stupid.

Fred smiled inside, his tension dropped a notch. Here was the information he was tasked to discover. Discord within the Italian family. This could be used by his patron, a man heavily intent on expanding his own power in this new and rich land.

Had Gino taken the time to ask some questions, he might not be so eager to hire his new front runners. Too arrogant to consider agendas directed by anyone but himself.

Mahmout's intensity, he took as lust for the women, strange he hadn't taken one, but that he put down to admirable professionalism, and attentive awe of his new employer.

Wrong on both counts.

Certainly Mahmout was lustful, but the arousing picture in his forehead was of the tight jeans encasing the backside of the young star striker as he led his chosen girl up the narrow staircase. While he enjoyed watching the pain and humiliation visited upon the girls, he recognised Gino for what he was. A useful fool in the enemy camp.

He had invited them in, paid them exorbitantly, and for the love of Allah, announced his traitorous intentions publicly.

What a fool. If no one else shot him, Mahmout might just do it as a public service.

A simple man, a boy to fuck, to please his cock, a Christian to shoot to please his God, and a pull on a hubble bubble to soothe his spirits at the end of the day. Simple pleasures.

Fred, a different kettle of fish.

Had he bothered to ask the obvious questions, so blatantly Arabic, three weeks in the country, named Fred?, even Gino may have smelt trouble.

Between the professional and the fanatic lies a gaping chasm, one which even a greedy fat-arsed car thief should spot. An accurate answer would have told him a lot. Rang some alarm bells.

As for Fred, well, he'd made his own decision. The glorious appellation his Mufti father had bestowed upon him, he would not utter in this nation of devil worshippers until the necessary social changes had been made.

The hours he'd spent in these halls of houris, filled him with a genuine fear for his immortal soul. Gino's announcements gave him ease, he was eager for more.

Discontent, greed, internal revolution, chaos in the offing, good times.

The Imam had explained and pre-forgiven some of the sinful horrors he may have to endure. The reality was far worse, but when he returned with this golden news he felt certain his soul would be safe.

A little less fanatical, and a little more professional and he may have noted Heather's hurried five -minute disappearance.

Mahmout hardly registered her at all, Gino thought she'd gone for more whiskey. That's what she told him the flashing light meant, "we will need more booze".

Roberto had reached Heather's door five minutes after Claudio had made Blues' acquaintance, he still vividly recalled the millisecond sight from the corner of his eye of a travelling brick, and the spray of blood and teeth. Some had almost stained his jacket. He was happy he could run fast, learnt to do that when he was young. Only fools stood up, when they could run away.

He'd deliver his message, that Brian might put up a bit of a fight, then grab one or two, Claudio didn't need one, of these sluts to fuck, while the fighting was going on. Plenty of willing young fellas, and the new guys as well, Gino was all tooled up. No one would miss him.

He was right, no one missed him.

Especially not Heather.

He pressed the bell again.

A stunning woman, Heather.

Six foot tall in heels, her red bronze mane adding more height. Black g-string and negligee, with generous lips and a sultry gaze.

A five-minute conversation with some jaded milksop husband could often cause complaint from fatigued employees, who endured the efforts she inspired. Most left hours later and considerably less solvent than originally planned, but always smiling, and they all came back.

Quarter of a century in the trade she knew all the tricks and most of her clientele's secrets, as well, her canny old boss supplied cameras and tapes to record interesting people. Money in the bank.

With an adult daughter nearing her degree, there was much she'd rather forget.

All scarlet and gold and milk white skin, Tony had hired and promoted her for her greatest asset, the grey bit that lived between her ears.

Fleet of mental foot, he reckoned, and again she proved his trust when the light from the street gate flashed.

"Fucking liquor light," feigning displeasure, "will need more booze, back in a minute".

She palmed her sap from beneath the counter, a gift from old Tony when he gave her the job, as she headed down the corridor, spied young Molly hiding in a nook and beckoned her to follow.

The urban centre, now tagged Potts Point, once knew a richer life.

With its cheek-by-jowl neighbour Kings Cross, it once formed the rich top to a long high escarpment. With rich soils and generously sunlit Sydney summers, its forests and hillsides all heavily timbered.

Where urban renewal and architectural design have not taken blight, the survivors and children of old forest giants still lined the leafy backstreets to this day. One sturdy old survivor, still standing, not five metres from the blind iron gate. He groaned and swelled, a hundred years now, extended a thick and heavy bow above Heather's tall stone wall, to throw shade into the soft grass of the small front garden. Shade pierced by day, here and there by sunlight, by night a single shaft of electric street glare. A coincidental, soft spotlight in the dark. Heather led Molly out the basement door, up the short flight of aged stone steps, and out across the lawn, stopped short in the electric bright spot.

A well-endowed young woman, having her halter top removed by the brothel madam before introduction to a customer, Molly would not usually consider unreasonable or unusual. But here, now?

"Chin up darling, shoulders back, it'll all be over in a minute."

Chilly, confused and a little concerned was Molly, but the girl had good reason to trust her boss and well knew it. She arched her back, lifted her chin and allowed long slender legs to drift slightly apart.

"How's that?"

Heather smiled and chuckled "you're a good one Molly" she spun, threw the girl's skimpy top into the thick hedge which lined and softened the walls of her garden, then stepped smartly to the gate.

Not a bad effort, in heels, at night, on grass, forty something or not, she flowed. Mind as fluid as her still graceful body, she quickly grasped the reality. Thought to herself, 'Brian won't be ringing the doorbell, gotta be a citizen, or one of Tony's boys. This should slow him down long enough to work out which is which'. Best be quick, if he keeps pushing that button, even that fat dill downstairs is going to realise that something's not right. She lifted the latch and allowed the heavy iron door to swing open.

Just one look was all it took. The clothes, the chains, the smug, arrogant, body language. Gotta be one of Tony's. He was in a hurry, and began to push past, she twisted slightly and allowed his right hand to graze her extended left breast. The sudden warmth and softness slowed him a touch, as she continued her pivot, leaving Molly exposed.

Lifted chin, generous mouth, upthrust perky breasts, long toned legs, slightly parted, whispering welcome. He stood gobsmacked, mouth hungrily agape, itching eager hands frozen waist high, tunnel vision, supreme, while Heather continued to turn.

Left foot back and across, hip twist, shoulder follow, right arm swung in a tight, hard arc, just like Nick taught her. The six inch shot-filled leather sap looped to her right hand caught him the length of his left temple. If shot, he'd have dropped no quicker.

He'd promised himself he'd leave Heather's well fucked.

With fractured skull and bleeding brain he was right.

Now it was Molly's turn to stand surprised, she'd heard iron in Heather's voice more than once, but lead to the head was an unexpected twist.

Heather waved her forward to help, then bent to his belt. She released it, then re-buckled the leather around crossed ankles, pulled back the buttonless shirt and knotted elbows behind. Unconscious or not, he'd play no further part. With shoulders and knees wrapped in slender feminine arms the heavy inert form fought both women's efforts to shift and conceal their handiwork.

The long bow above creaked and lifted as ninety kilos of silent black-wrapped Englishman vacated his perch, settled gracefully to earth at Heather's hip. A small breath of delighted recognition passed Heather's lips.

Jerry was early.

Molly's discarded halter appeared gently across her shoulder, the far end clasped loosely in leather-wrapped fingers. Brian had spotted her posed, as he'd first scaled the garden wall. So far he was enjoying the job. Hoped to enjoy it some more.

Mounted on 500cc trail bikes, using pathways and parks and little used byways, they'd rocketed across the city like two guided missiles. Even took a moment to stop at the club, introduced his best student, Brian liked his name, to prevent friendly fire, and check on the status of play. They passed Blues on the way. Watched him hijack a bus.

The two night fighters tucked the wasted thug between shrubbery and wall, then Jerry turned to Heather to share information.

Bus headlights coursed the street corner, sudden bright light through the still open gate. The girls tensed in alarm.

"Don't worry, that'll be Blues. Nick's on the way with a crew, Brian's about ready to go, he's got Tom and Jerry primed, he's got Bill the girl, and two of Nick's specials with him. Get back inside and turn the phone back on. When he calls, tell those arseholes he's on his way down with four guys. That's few enough to make 'em keen. You shouldn't have any trouble getting them all out in a bunch if they smell an easy win. We will part the bus right outside, box the bastards in, get the lot of them."

She brushed his jawline with her fingertips, his cheek with her lips.

"Done and done, catch you later."

Brian gave Molly a nod, then rescaled the wall, Jerry floated back to his bow and waited, spent a moment thinking about 'catch you later'.

Heather went back to work, eager to spring the trap.

Team Work

WHILE LIONEL KICKED BACK and considered Tony's invitation, Nick pointed Dave at the Darlinghurst cab rank, just outside the old Kings Cross snooker room, once upon a time a landmark venue. Smack in the middle of the Cross, this rank's drivers earned an education daily. Most of them armed against drunken attack and all of them up for anything with a quid in it. One of the drivers, a different kind of bloke named Terry, had a younger brother named Nick, he'd introduced him all around and now he was coming to visit. West from Double Bay, up Bayswater Road, work the tunnel flyover and onto the glitter strip.

With parking as always an impossibility, Nick gestured to a spot straight across from the cab rank.

"Drop me here. I'll rent some road block, meet you at Brian's ,and put your bookkeeper hat on. He will owe me a monkey when I get there."

"Five hundred for cabs! He won't like that."

One foot out the door Nick paused, allowed a little heat to show in his voice, "Look mate, tonight's all or nothing. We lose this one and we're all back in the pubs punching drunks, that's if we are still working at all, Brian knows that. We win, all tonight's going to cost him is tonight's bar takings, that's cheap for what he's buying, he knows that, too. Yes, he'll bitch, that's just for show.

Don't listen, just get the monkey. Tony started this to fuck Brian over, fucked if I'm paying to finish it".

He stepped out, "see you in a couple of minutes".

As the van moved off, the three silent riders began to bristle. Nick's tone, light and jocular the last half hour, had turned to sharp and short. With battle soon coming they followed his emotional lead. Nick stepped across the traffic-laden street as the passenger-filled front car moved away. Years of watching homeward-bound drunks debate possession of the next cab in line, a distraction he didn't need, moved him past the first three. He neared the driver's window of the fourth.

"G'day Billy," a friendly handshake protruded.

"G'day mate, you've just missed Terry, that was him pulling out. Gone for a pie."

"All good mate, probably better I missed him."

With a powerful, almost autistic penchant for high explosives and painful poisons, manufactured directly from your kitchen pantry, Terry could be a major asset. With a heavily jaundiced view of humanity, the result of too many drunken rear seat attacks, he could also be the king of collateral damage. Didn't care much for people, Terry. Best not taken to a brawl, you could win the battle and still lose all your soldiers.

While brother dear disappeared into the traffic, Nick laid out what he wanted.

"There's going to be some noise outside Heather's in about twenty minutes, could be a bit messy. Last thing I need is some citizen driving by and copping some of the flak."

The powers-that-be were always happy, and usually well paid to turn a blind eye when from time to time, the milieu decided, for whatever reason, to thin its ranks, but if Penelope Pureheart took a round through the passenger door while driving by, there would be hell to pay.

"Need some streets blocked off."

Billy's eyes tightened a touch, but the edge of his mouth betrayed his taste for an easy earn.

"'Round Heather's?"

From hundreds of drop offs, and when the tips were good, the occasional personal after-shift stress relief, the whereabouts of the house of good repute was no mystery to the boys on the rank.

"Yeah, no through traffic for about fifteen minutes, just gotta get the timing right. What do you reckon?"

Pursuant to his trade, Nick had developed friendships with some of the city's top barristers. In conversation after conversation, the two pieces of free advice never changed.

The first being "say nothing until I get there".

And the second, even more useful, "never ask a question if you don't already know the answer".

He almost smiled at Billy's reply.

"Victoria narrows at the end so one ought to block that. Grant and Saint Nim are all two way, you'll need a couple each there. Five all up, I reckon."

Having spent the last thirty seconds sorting notes, Nick passed five one hundred dollar bills across the driver's shoulder.

Billy eyed the bills and did a double take.

"How long you want us there?'

Nick did a quick count.

5 mins to get to Brian's

5 mins to sort the transport and give Heather the head's up.

5 travelling

5 to line 'em up

5 to bash 'em

5 to fuck off,

"half hour if you round 'em up now."

"Fuck, yeah!"

A hundred bucks each for a half hour of parking?

Billy knew just the boys. He pictured them each as he slid the folding into his top shirt pocket. Unlike some other uniform wearing locals, he'd make sure all his workers got their fair share.

Nick slid out the back seat and headed to the office. He could have made it in two, might of kept three up his sleeve.

Past the handybank fishermen.

"Hey Nick!'

"Hey boys," with a nod and a short wave he stepped to walk on past.

"Hang on bro!"

His knees bent the weight coming onto the balls of his feet, thinking.

'What? They're gonna try to rob me?'

"We been waiting for you!"

The family-sized brown hand disappeared into the pocket of a surprisingly stylish jacket, emerged not encased in the expected knuckle duster but holding a handful of hundreds. Six of them.

"Those boys was loaded bro! We got chains, watches, bracelets, clothes, cocaine! One big fucker too! Stevie got a new pair of shoes!"

A gap-toothed smile lit the shaded wall near two metres from the ground, an enormous pair of new white Nikes lifted for inspection one at a time. From the size of both smile and shoe, Nick could see what a rare and happy event this had been to young Stevie. The remark about the cocaine seemed self evident as well, perhaps also the cause of this sudden pecuniary generosity. But who the fuck were these boys, and why were they giving me money? From sometimes painful experience Nick surely did believe in karma, but this quick? And with a twenty percent profit?

This was worth two minutes.

His new mate needed no prompting to talk.

"Micky and Big Jay over the door said them nightclub boys were a present from you. We got heaps, we want you to have half the cash, we'd be a good team!" Nick pocketed the bills.

"That we would son, if you can keep to belting just the right ones."

"If you got enough right ones we can."

"Fair enough. Bit busy tonight, catch you in a couple of days, we will have a chat."

"Catch ya then bro."

The boys slipped away as quietly as they could. That is, not very. Nick spent two minutes more at the club front door. Came across a trim young Filipino, politely but earnestly assuring the two dubious ambience adjusters he really was wanted inside. A stranger in these parts, and not one to share secrets, he was loathe to drop Nick's name.

"Hey Justin, you scary big black bastard, what are you doing monstering my little mate? He's a dancer mate, good bloke."

Standing in their customary debating positions, one in front, one ninety degrees to the side, both monsters relaxed.

The timing was good.

Nick had a fair handle on the would-be thespian's personality. He had said, however regretfully, that he would be there. Another few moment's delay by the boys out the front may well have found them concerned owners of a dozen or so new body orifices.

A man of his word was Fuji. The moment passed.

Wide smiles and handshakes all round.

Nick slipped Micky a C note, he knew Justin would get 50.

"Mate of Nick's? Why didn't you say so son, come on in."

As they filed in, Fuji first, eyebrows asked the question 'dangerous? Him?'

Nick's eyes rolled in reply "Oh yeah!".

Further introductions continued inside.

The McCoys had arrived arm in arm with Bill, a walk-up start for any night club, especially this one. Both guardsmen held a power of respect for the stand up blonde.

She pointed and ushered her unfamiliar charges into Brian's office then headed downstairs to collect the owner, he had a safe down there with 'bang' things in it. Some of them made by Terry, some holding bullets. Tom and Jerry on their way from the bar, Cheryl behind carrying drinks. Nick slid into a recently vacated well-padded chair. Fuji broke into a grin, joked a grimace at Nick, then back slapped and swapped blasphemous banter with the sea-going brothers. Nick's nomadic crew were not unknown to each other.

Two large concerned citizens broke through the crowd and reached the office, with Bill and Brian hard on their heels, the small room filled quickly.

Cheryl placed the tray, slid Nick a wink and a slip of paper, "from Cherry," naming the good mate bar manager of young Tony's watering hole.

While the still-grateful girl squeezed out past Robbie's back, Nick flipped the slip of paper to read the hastily scribbled note. 'Three guns, Gino plus two,' was all it said. That was plenty.

Nick cracked a grin.

"Ahh, wheels within wheels, gotta love it."

The sisterhood had come through again.

Always in attendance, usually ignored, the smart bar girls kept their ears open and their mouths shut. The good ones became friends of Cheryl's.

Brian slipped a clip into the handle of a 22 calibre Colt, slapped the butt to lock it.

Got everyone's attention.

He screwed a short silencer onto the hollow end and threw out his first question.

"Right, what have we got?"

The question was thrown to the room. All eyes turned to Nick.

He'd already done his headcount.

"Seen anything of Jerry?"

"Yeah, him and a mate, Brian, skinny long-haired bloke, they're up on Heather's wall, took out one of Tony's runners about ten minutes ago. She's got the phones back on too."

"Where's Blues?"

"Ahh, bit of a change of plan there. He stole their bus. Got it parked out the front."

Half a dozen throats barked in laughter.

"Clever fuck. Good on him, that will help. Oh yeah, reminds me, Dave tell ya you owe me a monkey?"

"Yeah, what's that shit?"

"Got five cabs blocking any drive throughs."

"Yeah, alright, how long's that gonna last?"

"Time they are in place, about another half hour, should be plenty, if Heather can get them outside."

"She'll be right, smart woman that one. We best get going."

He threw out his second open question.

"Weapons? That fat Gino's down there, got a couple shooters with him."

"Three guns, Gino's carrying too."

Brian paused, thought to question Nick's information, then didn't. In answer to Nick's interruption the crew whispered a mutual 'yes!' Drowned out by a more enthusiastic reply from Bill, "Just once, I hope that fat fuck grows the balls to have a go!"

Tom grinned at Jerry as they both reached into underarm slings.

Nick missed which one spoke, focussed more on the guns produced. Lupras. Double-barrelled 12 gauge shotties. Pistol gripped with amputated barrels, a Sicilian weapon the boys had adopted with glee. Their beauty lay in their flexibility, eight ball loads great for opening locked doors, solid shot man killers or tonight's loads, one barrel bird shot, only probably fatal, and one barrel painfully effective rock-salt. A good terror weapon but loud, heavy too.

Brian's stunned brain did a back-flip, scrabbled to send a message to his mouth.

Nick was quicker.

"Cannons, fuck that! Most of these soccer boys got no idea what's going on."

He pointed to Brian.

"He spent a coupla grand to keep this quiet, you let those things off half the city will hear it. Sure, take 'em, but don't cock the fucking things, last resort only. Just bash 'em over the head with the metal bit. We'll take the shooters. Fuji, What have you got?"

The quiet Filipino opened his velcro-fastened jacket to reveal two rows of short, heavy, surgically sharp throwing knives.

"Right, I've got my pen, and I'm sure the boys on the wall will be loaded with shuriken, Jerry never leaves home without them."

Tom offered a derisive snort.

"Knives to a gunfight? Yeah good!"

"Look, if anybody absolutely has to be dead, Brian's got his needle threader. Collaterals we don't want. Hurt yes, bigly, but not dead. We'll have you two, Brain, Dave and Blues rush 'em from the front of the bus, you can be sure Gino won't be first out."

This got a knowing laugh.

"This five," pointing to his own crew, "they'll hit him from the back. Soon as we get there, you and Kev boost me and Fuji up onto the roof of the bus. When the shooters appear, they'll be looking for Brian, won't step out just blazing away. We will fill 'em full of darts and jump on the fuckers. We'll have four in the middle and five from each side. Bash 'em good."

To all but the two disappointed would-be artillery men, the plan seemed solid. For that little bit extra Nick turned back to Brian.

"Still got that searchlight you took off Justin?"

An ultra-powerful fisherman's spotlight come emergency beacon. Throw a solid beam of light three hundred metres. Blind a man a good five minutes with just a single flash. Jolly joker Justin had been having just a little bit too much cruel fun, got it confiscated by the boss. Nick could see how it might come in handy.

"Ok, here we go."

He continued to the club owner. "Call Heather, we will be there before she gets 'em all out."

They split to leave, front door and back.

Nick noticed the lump in Robbie's pants and threw him a look.

"They were great tits Nick."

"Yeah, but they belong to Cheryl mate. She's way too valuable to spend on a fuck. Keep it in your pants a while longer."

"Been at sea six weeks Nick."

"Look mate, these guys aren't cheap. Do the business right at Heather's, and we will all be back at Peaches for a piss up and freebies. They'll have the place back together enough and the girls do love a white knight."

"Free hookers and piss? And get paid?"

"YES, mate."

"Why are we waiting here?"

Nick smiled, always did appreciate enthusiasm, "we are not."

The gentle blood-warming five minute jog saw the two groups merge from darkened alleys across from the troubled bordello. A large tour bus obscured the gate. A quick, shielded flash from up in the adjoining tree said hello and showed him the location of his sharp eyed, black-wrapped, point men. Broad-beamed torch in one hand, Nick threw a vertical flash of his own in reply. He took two steps before the after image from high in the foliage began to gel. A black boot and a blue corduroyed leg wrapped around the trunk, three feet further, a small hand holding a briefcase hugged the timber.

No, not a briefcase.

Something somewhere between subconscious and memory told him 'no sweat, all good', no time for distractions anyway. He had learned long ago not to double guess his gut, snapped back to now, just a half a step sharper.

He signalled Brian to give Blues the news and waved Kevin and Tom to give him and Fuji the boost. While the boys were still breaking onto formation Heather had won the first round.

Took the call in clear line of sight, back turned, she took the one word message leaving and began to play with the would-be brothel owner's mind.

"He's coming here?" she waited two breaths.

"How many?"

Another two breaths then sent her surprised last query down the now empty line.

"No guns?"

Along with the words she also gave Gino a lesson in how an experienced actress can sell a fat greedy fool a convincing story without even looking at him.

Slight shifts in posture, muffled sigh, shuffled feet, shoulders slumped, then slowly squared, accepting new rules. She even looked smaller, slightly bent at the waist as she turned to give him the news.

"Brian's coming down to try to throw you out. He's got at least four guys with him but no guns."

"That's better, bitch."

He thought briefly about taking his belt to the loosely clad breasts hanging just beyond arm's reach, but that would be later, while she was apologising for her prior attitude.

"Tell your sluts to send the boys down."

She turned to the row of core buttons holding her laughter deep and thought a happy thought.

"That dumb, fat fuck. Send him out that full of careless confidence and he will be chopped meat for Brian and Nick."

As she flicked the room lights to signal times up, Gino laid out his master plan to his two on loan shooters.

"Fucking idiots, got no guns, but they probably got bats. We will send the boys out first then while they're fighting you can just pick him off."

Fred and Mahmout noted the lack of "I" or "me" in the plan, but expected no different, just a meaningful fact to be later reported.

Gino got his A team together.

In all the history of natural selection never a dopier, drunker, or more exhausted herd of sheep ever lined up to attack a hungrier pride of lions. The girls had done their part with knowing vigour and alcoholic generosity.

Out in the courtyard to drum the battle blood and count aloud the coming victories, drunks are boastful as well as off balance.

"Yeah, fucked her brains out. Gonna bash these cunts then go give her some more."

Gino at the back yelling orders.

"Quiet, shut up! He will be here any minute, don't let him hear ya, stay quiet. Wait 'til he rings the bell then Fred will pull the gate open then charge the bastard."

The crews set in ambush heard all of his words and most knew the light lit inside, so Bill took the cue and banged a fist on the gate.

"It's Brian, let me in!"

One slightly less-befuddled drunken hero noted the tone. "He sounds like a girl! Bash the poof."

Out the wide -flung gate and across the dark footpath, to confront a dark blank bus wall.

The trio of shooters stood hard on their heels.

Three things at once confusing enough, but the sun bright beam proved a stunner.

"Oi" from the front.

"Ai" from the rear.

Heads swivelled, eyes stretched, the ambush crew's eyes, pre-warned, jammed shut.

"GO!"

Mahmout was quick, had the pistol half raised before darts and throwing stars grew out of his chest and shoulder. The gun hit the ground as Brian's boot hit his head.

Fred did nothing.

Gino had panicked.

He never intended to fire a shot, just a hand on the butt as it hung in its sling. Reckoned it made him look scarier, and if you don't pull it out, no-one will shoot you and you won't go to jail, reckoned it made him smart. Safety catch? Too macho for that.

Sudden burning bright light in his eyes, sudden pain in his big bicep, a squeeze of the hand, the erupting round scared him shitless.

Did Fred no good as well. Big calibre bullet through the bottom of his spine, ended all of his fun right there. Began his new career. Bile-filled, wheelchair bound fundamentalist preacher. Hatred and frustration to fill his days, his last walking memories, breasts and bums, bright light and crippling pain to plague his nights. Suited him quite well.

Gino crashed back through the gate.

"Bastard! Coward!"

One player had spied his escape. Enraged by his tour guide's sudden departure, Mario sought to vent. A dark shape, furious in motion, dropped a man on his right, made a hole, revealed his attackers.

He screamed his defiance and charged the centre.

Made Lionel's job easy.

One made to order, six foot South Auckland right hand. Bang in the middle of his forehead. Broke no bones, not even any blood, but knocked the boy colder than ice cream in winter time.

He'd already dropped two, and this one was the special. He figured the mixed crews could well handle what was left of the opposition. So the body went over one shoulder as he turned and headed south. Obvious enough where Nick would have placed the cabs, he thought to use one.

Leapt together from the top of the bus, Fuji and Nick hit the pack in the centre, fists and feet then knives for a moment. One caught Nick across the ribs, the arm drew back for another slash before Fuji's left hand blade caught the tendon. The wielder screamed quite loudly before Bill kicked his head.

Demoralising, that short-cut scream.

Especially to follow surprising and disastrous gun play.

Survivors offered surrender, an offer Brian accepted, once all were unconscious.

"Grab watches and wallets, there's too much to hide with that fucking cannon going off, there will be ambos and news crews here in ten minutes. The coppers can't keep 'em out. Let 'em call it a gang fight, a robbery."

He thought to ask, "Anyone hurt?"

His query got no's all around, but from Nick.

"Wouldn't ya fucking know it? Just fucking me!"

A neat three-inch slice he held closed with his left hand.

"I better get to Vinnie's, get this stitched." 'Yeah right, ok the rest of you split. We will meet at Peaches in an hour. Sort out the wages. Where's Lionel?"

"Don't worry, I'll take his, we are having breakfast together."

This drew a look.

"Yeah, ok. See you at Peaches."

"See you there."

"See you there."

WAGES OF SIN

WHILE BRIAN GAVE DIRECTIONS, Jerry slid back behind the curtain wall. Gino, flat on his breathless fat arse, made it to the bottom of Victoria Stairs, a steep, stone one-hundred metre 19th century creation. They fall from the back of Kings Cross all the way down to the Woolloomooloo docks, ending just opposite Harry's Cafe De Wheels, an old tricked- up caravan come diner renowned by seamen worldwide, home of the floater, pie and peas, that is, Terry's favourite late-night snack.

"Gotta get rid of this fucking gun."

Couple of years before, Tony bought a fishing boat. Nominally for public charter, in reality reserved for guys in the know. A handy asset. Gino looked at the waters of Woolloomooloo Bay, and remembered.

"Perfect, no one will find the fucking thing twenty miles out to sea. Good place for me to be too. Blame Brian for the shooting. Perfect."

Blood-soaked right sleeve, he stumbled across the street, spotted a driver who had just finished his pie, heading back to his cab.

"Oi! Rose Bay?"

"Get in."

'Round to Garden Island then up the hill, Roslyn Gardens, Bayswater, then South Head Road. Halfway through Double Bay still struggling with his jacket.

"What the fuck? What's this?"

A hard nub, steel, sticking through the bicep. Tug, pull, aaarrrgh! as it came out. Pain.

"A pen, a fucking pen!" razor sharp and unusually heavy, he didn't notice.

He cursed and threw it in the front seat.

Attacked from the rear more than once, Nick's brother jumped in his seat.

Gino saw it and snorted.

"It's just a pen ya sook, keep it," the insult made him feel better, just like a tough guy.

Terry was surprised, he'd only ever seen one like it once before.

"Turn in here, that wooden boat shed."

He pulled out a fifty.

"Keep the change, I wasn't here."

The fare was forty.

If he wasn't such a cheap fucker he might have saved his own life.

Terry looked at the blood-spotted note, then the blood-spattered back seat, thought to himself "yes you were asshole, that'll take me a half hour to clean up".

He rang Leslie to say he'd be home early then headed back to base to start scrubbing.

Nick had his own problems.

Saint Vincent's Public Hospital, Casualty Ward, two hundred metres from Oxford Street, two hundred metres from the Cross. Saturday Night.

He presented with a three-inch slash wound to the abdomen, was greeted with a wry, knowing smile, handed a folded swab to staunch blood flow and a patient identification form to fill in. Told to take a seat while serious cases were attended to. Another ordinary Saturday night.

He was halfway down the page of misinformation when the first of his former dancing partners was carried in. His porters walked straight past the seated guy with his face turned to the paperwork.

Nick made a mistake.

Perhaps the pain, perhaps just carelessness, he glanced up as the second group limped past.

"That's him, that's the little guy!"

Up fast. Right fist to the chin of the first guy, left heel through the knee of the second.

Run!

"Too many of them, on my own, specially while I'm leaking. Not out the front, that's straight into the rest of them."

The sliding glass doors giving access to the treatment cubbies were opened only by the push buttons behind the nurse's station.

A quick wink to Dianne and a subtle nod saw the attending matron slide sideways on her wheeled desk chair. A two-step diving vault saw him through the narrow chest-high aperture. But for the blood spray and deep grimace of pain, it could have been quite graceful.

Xavier woke on his tucked-away, just out of sight stool, to spot Nick roll across the office floor and push to his feet.

"Oargh, Jesus! That didn't do my side any good, definitely need a stitch in that."

"G'day Nick."

"G'day Xave."

Previous customers, drunk, drug fucked or just plain nasty, had demonstrated a genuine need for night-time security to protect the health workers, so the hospital's human resources hired one of Nick's guys. The sweetly polite half mokued one hundred and forty kilo grandson of axe-wielding Polynesian cannibals took the one long step necessary for his massive chest to cover the nurse's window, looked out on the room filling with pre-damaged angry boys, now standing very still and looking back at him and inquired gently across his shoulder.

"Problem bro?"

"No mate, just passing through."

"Have a good one bro, I'll be here."

Thanks mate, you too."

Nick knew his way.

Between routine pit stops for running repairs, and numerous clandestine tours guided by the lovely Leslie, senior theatre nurse, committed junkie, long-time live in lover and perfect soul mate to a brother who had surrendered to heroin a decade before, the block-long public hospital's labyrinth byways were warmly familiar to the bleeding escapee.

Left, down the corridor forty meters, right, through the orderlies' stockroom. Grab a dustcoat. Down, right again through the boiler room, up, left, through the laundry dock, across the street and into the darkened recesses of Green Park. In close around the rotunda, drape the dustcoat over the homeless kid sleeping under the bench, then across Darlinghurst road to the Wall.

An unconscious snort and a shake of his head. Half pity, half disgust as the hot-pantsed teenage boys lined against the imposing convict stone work of Sydney's District Court, flaunted their wares to the off-duty doyens of city society as they cruised slowly past in their BMWs and Mercs.

Just looking for love.

Cheap as possible of course.

One of the boys sported a crenellated wig, cleverly purloined from the back seat while sucking some fat barrister's skinny dick in the front, advertising of a sort.

Nick paused in his rush, took stock of the moment and cursed himself with vigour. Changed plans on the run.

"Stupid, might be from out west but of course they'd of headed to Vinnies'. Should have thought of Leslie straight away. She'll be fine for a couple of stitches."

His clandestine visits had invariably ended in a stockroom. The apartment she shared with her beloved cab driver now choc to bursting with variously flavoured ampoules, and a hotch-potch of medical supplies.

"Sure to have a bent needle and some thread somewhere in the house."

North on Darlinghurst one hundred metres, down the short stone steps, left through the gate and up the outside staircase. He expected a noisy effort would be needed to wake the sleeping health worker.

Surprise!.

The door flew open at his second knock. Surprising also the less than concealing lingerie, less suprising the clouded eyes, slurred speech and loaded syringe in her left hand.

"Nick! Fuck! I thought it was Terry."

"It's only two o'clock girl, his shift don't finish till three."

"He's coming home early, some asshole bleeding all over his back seat."

Her eyes slowly let in some more light.

"You bleeding! Was it you?"

"No girl, not me, but that is what I want to see you about. You up for some sewing?"

Spurred by the blood dripping onto the front step her mind cleared just a touch.

"Yeah, yeah, come in get your shirt off and get on the table. I'll get a needle and some rum. Wanna shot?" She proffered the loaded pick.

"No thanks girl, just the rum. Night's not over and it looks like breakfast is going to be busy. Matter of fact, you got any uppers, I'm starting to fade a little."

He slipped his shirt off, eased back onto the kitchen table. Leslie reappeared fully stocked. Benzadrine tablets, bent needle, dissolvable thread and a bottle of dark rum. Bundaberg's finest.

Due to one or two unfortunate incidents Nick had barred himself from drinking the stuff years before, but as a wound cleanser, God knows what kind of shit might have lived on the slashing edge, it remains the peerless antiseptic, does sting a bit though.

The first two stitches went in well.

By the third, the energy generated by his surprise visit had begun to grow thin and Leslie's opiate of choice again began to make its presence apparent.

As her spine arched forward and her hands began to forget what they were doing Nick gave the now near-somnolent nurse a nudge.

"Focus, Les!"

She woke with a start, and a jerk.

"Ow."

"Sorry."

Stitches four and five flowed smoothly, six was slower, she snapped back awake at seven as the front door swung open to reveal her bloody-handed cab driver home early for his knock-off shot.

The near-estranged brothers swapped queries. Explanations followed as Leslie finished her sewing.

"This would be yours then, thought it looked familiar."

He displayed the disguised steel dart.

"Where is he?"

"Gone fishing."

With the amphetamine beginning to kick in Nick no longer felt any great need to be lying down.

He swapped a fifty to ransom his pen.

 "Thanks mate."

Left another on the table for the panel beating.

"Thanks again guys, gotta get going, places to be, people to see. See you again soon."

He was ignored, there was dope to shoot and money to buy more. Just a short walk back to Peaches, but long enough for a quick self-satisfied sit rep.

"Must be doing something right, karma's starting to work my way for a change. Know exactly where that fat fuck is, till midday at least."

The brothel door eased open as he reached to press the buzzer.

"Looks like someone's been waiting for me, this could be fun."

Like any other night the door opened to reveal an attractive young woman. Unlike other nights this one was fully clothed.

"Molly?"

Nick was nonplussed. While not overly familiar with all the staff, he knew the reticent young worker to be a particular favourite of Heather's and rarely, if ever, seen far from her side. Finding her at Peaches was a one-off.

"Hey Nick, just waiting for Brian."

It had taken him two years to get her story, another one before she told it herself. They were vaguely friendly.

"Bit early girl, he'll still be scraping the wages together."

The girl's sudden interest in the battling club owner surprised him. Never thought of her as a ladder climbing star fucker.

He added with a light laugh, "probably hoping they're having so much fun they'll forget about getting paid. Bit of bad luck about Bill."

She dropped her voice. "Not him, silly. Brian the ninja."

"Where'd you get that name?"

"Jerry told me."

That rocked him. For his professionally invisible mate to give his own name was astounding, to give his mate's was unthinkable. Real concern framed his next question.

"And how the hell did you get his name?"

"Heather introduced us."

Nick heard a penny drop. Months of surreptitious looks and stymied gestures suddenly made sense.

"Brian?"

Even in the sparse light he could see the oh-so-expensive courtesan redden. Amazing.

Offered a little voice of experience.

"You do know while you're working it can never be real."

Molly liked guys with long hair, liked guys who dressed in black, particularly liked guys who'd drop from the sky and crush her tormentors underfoot.

"Dad's up for parole in two months."

She was sweet sixteen when her mother's brothers introduced her to sex, drugs and alcohol. Not in a good way. Men in their forties.

She was seventeen when her father was sentenced, when the rest of the family, in shame, anger and ignorance turned their backs on the too rapidly maturing young woman.

Notwithstanding his plea of mitigation in the eyes of the law, as a double murderer dad would spend a large lump of his lagging in Long Bay Jail.

She packed her bags and moved to Sydney town, the once upon a time academic dreams and teenage fads all now replaced with a passionate pecuniary pursuit.

Studied all the ads, asked a lot of questions before she knocked on Heather's door. Dad now had one hundred well-watered acres and a brand new farmhouse to come home to. She'd worked real hard, achieved all she dreamed, bit of a bonus if she could take home a good man herself.

Daddy always told her you could pick a man from his mates.

This guy's mates were out of the box.

"Brian know about this?'

"Not yet."

"How about you head back to your place, it's liable to get untidy in here. I'll collect the wages and send them down with his and Jerry's. Perhaps you could surprise him, pleasantly. He'd like that."

Molly smiled, half a giggle, "Perhaps".

She leant forward, kissed him on the cheek.

"Thanks, Nick."

Nick felt the grin in the corners of his lips. Happy. He let it spread.

"Looks like Brian's days of punching drunks are just about over."

A short sharp stab of almost envy. He brushed it aside.

"Bloody nice, but not my road."

He trod down the dim corridor and pushed through the thick sound curtain into the oversized waiting room.

Light and laughter, booze and thick lines of coke, the occasional girl sporting a newly blackened eye, one or two fat lips. No one unhappy as the post-fight stories flowed.

"What's all this?"

He beckoned to the long low sometime coffee table sometime mini dance floor and the watches, chains, wallets and assorted bling strewn across it.

Blues, Jack Daniels in one hand, a peach-shaped buttock in the other, answered with a grin.

"That robbing them idea of Brian's was a beauty. We got over five grand there in folding, some of the bling's shit but most of it is good and most of these naughty boys were carrying baggies. There was almost a half ounce of blow."

Nick considered, that was a lot of money in nose candy. Unlikely the boys would have paid for it themselves. Went a long way to explaining their continued bad manners. He spotted an angry fat lip on Robyn and forgot about forgiving them. Fuck 'em.

He raised an eyebrow to Blues.

"Was?"

Blues smiled an innocent smile.

"Coupla the girls were feeling a little hard done by, they're better now."

He gave the buttock a gentle squeeze, got a playful tongue in the ear by way of reply.

"And there's still a dozen odd grams left, just waiting for everyone to arrive before we split it all up."

Nick's eyes swept the room again.

Blues in the armchair, Tom at one end of the couch set next to it and partner Jerry at the other, with free drinks flowing and their favourite ladies ensconced on warming laps, the two oversized mates were well prepared to wait. Kevin sat near, enjoying enthusiastic introductions, looking like nothing so much as a happy young lion, great mess of tawny hair, eyes all a-goggle and tongue hanging out. Kid in a candy store.

Fuji was slow dancing, no music, just quietly da dut da dahing out time as he led each girl in turn with a light touch to hip or shoulder, he loved to teach. Soon he would make his choice. No rush, a man who enjoyed his foreplay.

Bill in the far corner, deep in conversation with Lady Di, the starkly beautiful leather-clad hard-arsed veteran, number one on the roster and soon for promotion, and two of her bruised young co-workers. Their lips were thick but stretched in mirth as she recounted their proxied revenge.

Still possessed of that unique slow motion perception ever emergent when death rides close, she gave them hard fists and a blade, silver-capped toe piece deep in the balls, an angry heel weighted with malice driven to the back of the skull, face crushed into footpath, a frighteningly violent mother hen.

The girls adored her.

Then there was Dave.

He had chosen the two-seater couch for himself, more room for the girls to compete. The silly young ones did just that.

"This hard-bodied Adonis must be the boss, he took the biggest chair, and he's wearing a Rolex."

They battled it out. A sly breast gently here, a buttock caressed thigh, greedy fingers gently questing, searching out and stroking imaginary aches and injuries. No idea of teamwork or reality, each soon to become the pampered gangster's moll of their teenage dreams. Or perhaps not.

To keep them whetted, and much to Nick's chagrin, Dave occasionally laid claim to further violent revenge possibly not all his own doing.

Nick near cringed as he thought to himself "Jesus wept, they should all be wearing fucking L plates. And he's still got almost as much to learn as them. Fucking sad."

And then out loud to Di.

"Where's the boss?"

"She went down to Vinnies to see Eric, Bill said you went there, too. Didn't you see them?"

"No, didn't stay long enough. There was a crowd when I got there."

He turned to Dave.

"How about the brothers? I thought they would be here for sure?"

He sat open mouthed , not sure how to respond as choking chortles reared from the couches and a stern look speared from Bill.

"What?"

Kevin recovered first.

"Lionel took a cab somewhere, said 'see ya tomorra' so Bill and I came with these two, pointing to his two new cartoon character mates. We thought we were a little bit early but those boys were here ahead of us. Funny as. Toes tapping, fingers drumming on the table. Soon as we walk in its 'Gooday, see you later'. Grabbed the closest girl, both of them, threw her straight over the shoulder and ran for the stairs. Got exactly that evil look from toe caps over there."

He gestured to Bill.

"Anyway, the skinny one's seen it and stopped just for a second, looked her straight in the face and tried to make it all good."

In unrehearsed unison all on the couches broke in.

"Been at sea six weeks Bill!"

Then collapsed as a group back into laughter and self indulgence, even Bill struggled to hide an unbidden smile.

"Just Brian with the money and your two sneaky mates to get here."

"Blues?"

"Ever met his missus? He's gone home mate. Just your boys and Brian."

"I know where one is, fairly certain he won't be coming, I know I wouldn't with what he's got on offer, the other, I got an idea where he might be, wouldn't be expecting him in here though, just a little bit too public for him."

He nodded to indicate the girls.

"Not real keen on people who don't know when to shut up. I'll take theirs, Lionel's too, be seeing him a bit later."

The comment didn't raise an eyebrow, knew him too well to consider theft any part of his plan.

"Expect Brian will be here any minute."

By the time Nick poured himself a drink, he was.

Possessed of his own key the nightclub owner made his presence known as he pushed through the heavy sound curtain. The loot on the table the first thing to catch his eye.

Nick passed him a fresh poured Jack then turned to pour himself another while he deciphered the look in his mate's eye.

"Not thinking about discounting the wage bill are you? You know as well as the rest of us Eric put his hands up, on his own, against a coupla dozen shitheads. Won't ask for it himself but he's earned a full share, at least.

Split the rest of the folding between the girls with the lumps and bumps. They might be feeling okay just now but when the toot wears off they'll miss at least a couple of shifts before the bruises go down. Can't have them working looking like punching bags. I'll take the bling and I.D's. Pretty sure I know a bloke can work it back to the boys involved. Let them know how easy they are to find, let them know some of the bad things that can happen to people who talk too much. Betcha they'll be happy just to get this shit back. Carrot and stick stuff. Cheap insurance."

He took a thirsty swig of the hard liquor, lifted his empty hand and gestured to the private party just beginning to make steam.

"Be surprised if there's any candy left after this lot, if they don't finish it off the next shift will."

He delivered the statement deadpan, logic and ethic clear and accepted.

Brian began passing out packets of fifties.

"I'll take four of those."

The money passed without comment.

"Back in a minute, split that lot up for me will ya?"

Gold bits and wallets went in one pile, cash in another and marching powder spread across the table top in a thick party line. All imbibing, which, of course was everyone, found the coke particularly enjoyable, considering who paid for it, what for, and just who ended up having all the fun.

Lots of Ho Ho Ho.

Nick slid back up the hall and paused outside on the footpath.

Bright lights to the right from the neighbouring club, darkness to the left as the street grew residential. He scanned the avenue but did no good so tapped his head twice and stepped into a shadow, joined three heartbeats later by a dark narrow form.

"Jesus, you're getting good at that."

"Good teacher."

"Figured you'd be waiting for him to show before you stepped in."

"He's late."

"Good news, waiting's over, he's not coming."

Empathy is a good thing if you use it right, Nick had been working on it. He could feel the sudden tension and change in posture three feet away in the dark.

"Don't worry, all good, especially for him. Seems Heather's taken a shine to the bloody immigrant, he never left her place."

"Didn't see that coming."

Nick extended a hand, two rolls of bills and a plastic baggie in the palm.

"Yeah well, lots of surprises around Heather's tonight, there's a monkey each and something to help you keep your eyes open."

"Not for me thanks mate, long night, I'm straight to bed after I pay him."

"Good idea mate but take it anyway, who knows, you might thank me later."

They shook hands and parted, Nick amused, Brian confused.

He headed back to his traffic-scorning transport thinking about surprises, somehow sure he'd missed something. Nick headed back inside to his lodgings for the night, making plans for the coming day.

Down the hall and into the parlour, partook of the party toot, now a thin white line laid the width of the table, then stepped across to Bill and Lady Di.

"I need a good hot tub and a couple of hours lying down before we go."

He peeled off the blood-soaked shirt.

"What chance a clean one of these?"

"No problem, we got racks of clothes."

"Something in silk would be nice."

The leather-clad senior temptress turned to the girls sitting in fawning attendance and nominated a room.

"Take him up to number six, got that big shallow tub in it. Don't let him drown, and one of you throw those jeans in the wash, can't have him going to breakfast looking like he just came from the back of a butcher's shop."

The word breakfast raised his eyebrows and he turned his head to Bill.

"Well, gossip girl, seeing you're spreading the news perhaps you could organise a cab for us.'Bout six thirty?"

A small critique, well understood.

"Yes, sure Nick."

She used her small voice.

He used the rare leverage while it still had some life in it.

"And get some rest yourself, we're up early."

"Yes, Nick."

A nod from Di, the girls took one hand each and headed for the stairs. He paused for a moment for a quick word with Tom and Jerry, arranged to borrow their nondescript tote bag to carry the bling and things. Swapped see you laters then allowed himself to be led away for an hour or two of gentle spoil.

Thought to himself 'gotta get some sleep in too, brain's gunna need to be on its feet come morning'.

The Legend Of Tony O

THEY'D WAITED MONTHS IN hopeful disbelief.

In a moment, in a room, wizened eyes had seen each other.

Had seen in.

Could it be true? Someone that real in this world of shit?

Questions were asked. Quiet conversations with well-trusted friends. All good.

In the hot afterglow, battle lust not nearly spent, their first coupling came in a sprint. Strewn clothes, suddenly sodden sheets and interesting bruises to rise days later. Their second far slower and far more intense. With senses sharpened through years of vigilant residence, somewhere in the middle she felt Molly's return.

Subtle sounds, the one spare key in the old lock, the scrape of the heavy timber front door, a discreet familiar scent in the air.

Early.

Puzzling.

Pleasantly preoccupied for the moment, a puzzle she decided which could wait for its own answer.

As she glided still damp back from the ensuite shower, her newfound lover's eyes growing wide in fond memory and delighted anticipation, an already quietened engine burbled to silence in the rear service lane.

Puzzle solved.

Jerry sat up.

"That's Brian."

"Easy English, he'll get all the welcome he could ever wish. You'll just get in the way."

Most parts of the tall pommie relaxed, content to trust his mate's immediate future to the woman who knew best just how a man might like to be welcomed. With any luck that starlight angel from the front yard might be part of it.

She gestured to a rising tent in the sheet well suited to his stature.

"And put that thing away as well. Be poor form, and most impolite, to show up at Tony's breakfast table with my brains obviously fucked out."

"Tony! We just bashed his soldiers, now you're going to breakfast with him?"

"Not the idiot boy, the man. He's got a birthday for his grandson today, the boy Lionel stole. He wants a meeting first, me and Nick and a couple of others. Tonight's little shindig should put a hole in the idiot son's ambitions for the moment but it would be good to have a chat, see where we go from here. As long as that arrogant pig's on the strip there never will be any peace. Be a large mistake to show up sleepless and shattered."

"What the fuck! We been waiting months for this, now you're going to jump out of my bed and run off to some Italian pensioner. What is this shit? You, Nick, Brian, everyone treats the old fuck like royalty. And that shit about him being unkillable. You can't believe that.

Shot in the heart then gets up and kills the shooter by sticking a pool cue up his arse. That's gotta be horseshit."

Heather stopped at the bedpost, pondered a moment.

"Ever heard about Sheharzaad?"

"Arabian nights? A thousand nights of no sex? Fuck that!"

"A thousand nights, from your very own lips. But don't be mistaken my love, in case you've not noticed, and you certainly should have, I am as eager as you, not a thousand nights of rest, just what's left of this one."

A hard word there in her comment, it disturbed the once-determined bachelor. He glanced inside himself, found an echo to her emotion. More than her entreaties it quietened him some. Bugger, he found himself caring. Worse, he found that was ok.

"I do need to touch you, to taste your skin, so get over on your stomach and I'll rub your back and tell you a story. If we're going to work there's some things you should know. Everyone knows the legend, you should know the truth of it."

Piqued by the unfamiliar emotion growing in his stomach Jerry lazily complied.

She placed a knee on the bed then swung aboard to kneel across his lower thighs, gently placed the tip of her tongue a hand span above his butt crack and slowly lapped the sweat from the base of his spine. Practised fingers kneaded the twin towers of muscle embracing the vertebrae while the tips of her tits stroked gently behind. Heard a groan of delayed pleasure from beneath.

"Oooah, that's not fair."

"Patience, patience, all good things come to those willing to wait."

"Don't know about willing to wait but if that's what it's going to take, do get on with your story."

"Not my story, Tony's. Now, where was I before someone interrupted? Oh yes, royalty, why do we treat him like royalty? Well my precious, that would be because he is. Tony's family has been making the rules and feeding retainers for a thousand years and more. Unlike that jumped-up German family that changed its name to Windsor about a hundred years ago, yes, that's right, the ones you have lording it over in Old Blighty, Tony's line, an uninterrupted, direct descendant eldest son line, goes right back to when the Romans were starting to row up and down the Italian coast.

Probably further, if you listen to the way Fulvia tells it. Have you met Tony's daughter yet? Scary woman that one. She's the keeper of the family history, can recite the lineage right back to the original Padrone. He's still the family saint. Took his people out of North Africa, snatched them from sudden war, from death, conquest and slavery. Packed family, retainers and crews into three boats and slipped by night into the Mediterranean.

Storm punished, swept across an impossible reef they discovered the hidden bay that would become their new home.

Two boats survived, the wreck of the third also washed into the sheltered natural amphitheatre.

And the miracle part, nobody died.

While the men bored into the hill, the first crude shelter for the women and children, piled rock upon coral, and topped it with brush to pen the few sheep and goats, the refugee Prince studied the reef.

It could be done, it must be done.

Crop the coral finger, clear the rubble from the base of the cliff face, a deep and oblique channel was there, invisible from the sea, near inaccessible from land, in a lonely south coast corner of the island in the middle of the sea, in the middle of the world.

To work!

Three years.

Seeds and sprouts found abundant welcome in the rich virgin soils. A bloated vine trellis now spanned one slope, flourishing herd and flock now claimed the other.

Laden with produce and a handful of precious stones a new furbished trader slipped warily through the hard won channel.

Found a passing peace had erupted, found battle-hardened warriors now dressed as customs men and tax collectors. The ancient enemy now the Emperor's thieves.

Inherent repugnance for state sponsored thugs led them North by East. To broach, by sail and oar, those mysterious straits always in ebb and brave the dark sea beyond them.

To barter, to trade, to form new alliances and found new friendships. To return triumphant laden deep with dark timbers destined for the treeless south and rich thick furs for the Balkans in winter.

Friendships grew strong through the courage of sons, alliances entrenched through the marriage of daughters.

A grandson sailed west, his crew to peer through the pillars of Hercules, not yet to chance the unknown ocean, soon but not yet, then turned south and east to re-explore the ageing Padrone's once home coast. Unearthed old friends, discovered new ones.

By the time it took for Tony's turn to take the tiller, the network had grown vast.

To Venice in near north then up the rivers into the belly of Europe, from aunts in Odessa to cousins in Cairo and all the way to Ireland's Atlantic coast.

These latest Gaelic bonds forged by his own father as he and a crew half his own, half rebellious Fenian, offloaded small arms and bullets by the half ton in shady creeks and lonely bays the length of the western coast. Close escapes and tales of derring-do pub-sung across the Republic, as the Irish are want to do, brought his fame and his name to the powers that be.

A fame unwanted and forever to leave the family wary of British revenge.

They expected vengeance would be sought, for the Orsini clan vendetta framed life more potent than religion, more necessary than children.

A fame also surprisingly fruitful, new friends appeared, new ports of call, secret ones, the family favourites.

Cousins in Sebastapol sought sanctuary in the West.

A three step journey.

A reeking soiled scow with fish-strewn decks, nervous passengers crowded cheek by jowl crowding bilge and hull. A moonless night, a race through the Bosphorus blessing the tide, dodging armed, armoured and angry ships of war. Then home to revictual, rest the crew and tranship to the clan's newly bought flagship. A small coal burner, sturdy enough to brave deep ocean swells, small enough to grace narrow and shallow Irish streams.

Four days in a lonely barn then off to the promised land. American Odessa the usual goal.

Not this time.

Something new.

The spotter plane flew lower to investigate an unchartered harbour. A weather-beaten old lookout let both barrels go at the underside. The sudden shot turned all heads, rifle fire greeted his second pass. A hole in the wing, a hole in the floor.

The men cheered and backslapped as he flew off, confident in their victory.

Not so confident Tony's second daughter. Wise beyond her years, from her hidden eyrie she'd seen the ships of war steam past, many ships. Far distant in the sky, flying machines, like bees in swarm.

Now they would come.

She gathered the young ones and moved to the caves, the ancient sanctuary, cool and secure deep in the earth.

More new things.

Things called Stukas, things that shrieked from the skies with ugly bent crosses on their wings.

Some survived, the young ones Fulvia had taken to the bunker. Angelo's wife, wailing in grief, who lived long enough to bury her children before putting a shotgun in her mouth, a handful of heartbroken retainers. Eight sturdy young smugglers, their hearts aching for revenge.

With the dynasty destroyed only vengeance remained.

With an enemy possessed of steel ships and flying machines he needed an army.

Bit of bad luck the only one available was British, but no, there was another. In Tobruk, Australians.

They'd drunk his wine, eaten goat from his herd, and paid his captains well. Practical men,

honourable men, one in particular, a colonel. A hard man, risen from the ranks, admired   by his own men and trusted by Tony's. Smart enough to appreciate the treasure Tony carried in his mind, a lifelong smuggler's chart of the entire Mediterranean coast, and senior enough to attract the commander's attention.

With a crew of eager partisans already aboard he could gather and supply information, with arms and explosives he could kill.

Violence and politics, work for which he was well suited.

Fighting age men were offloaded, America now unreachable they'd pay their passage to a new southern home with gunfire and blood.

A country called Australia, a town called Sydney, strange names, but there were cousins there, fishermen, a safe harbour where the women could wait, where the children would thrive and more importantly, survive, while the dark work was done.

Time was needed, from servant to master he'd not leave Europe until there were none left to kill.

A deal could be done.

A deal would be done.

Non combatants were loaded, all the women and children, a few old men, the ten year old son of a once military man begged to stay and fight with his father. Would not leave without a blood-sealed pact, as long as Tony lived, so would his father, for his part Victor would swear to protect the children.

Angelo stayed to bury the dead while Tony, careless of detection, scudded south and west to barter for a new world. Now they were discovered their enemy would return. He had to be quick.

He found his colonel, a solid man with a hard past and a promising future.

A man who made surprising introductions. Not so much the beribboned brigadier set quietly in his corner, his one contribution being to bar the delivery of British small arms into the hands of 'wogs', no, more the mysterious men in mufti. Powerful men from shadowy places, men with lists of targets, truckloads of captured weapons, small high powered explosives and another thing, a radio, a new thing, something to take direction, report the results of his vengeance and plot re-supply.

With gunnels awash from a hold crammed with murderous iron they slunk back to their shattered cove.

Found a dozen angry men amidst new lain graves and two small boats refloated.

Laden and grim the forlorn flotilla slipped their home channel for the last time.

To a bolthole prepared ages before, a refuge to which to retire, to heal wounds, to plot, to plan, to recharge and go again.

Vengeance proved inspirational, carried the men almost gleefully through two years of hell.

In years of peace a good man can strive a life-time for prominence, in times of war it can be much quicker.

Tip toe raids and knives in the dark, explosives blinding bright in the night, bullet-riddled hulls and searchlights on the sea.

They came to bless the Brigadier bigot.

With only the sound of captured Wehrmacht small arms to locate a target, a somewhat dangerous and typically audacious tactic quickly emerged. Two men would infiltrate the lines and let loose in both directions, then scurry away while the enemy decimated itself with startled crossfire.

Made 'em cranky, that one did.

Tony soon came to see the value of his work, helped largely by the high price put on his head by the Reich, he had become famous to his friends, infamous to his enemies; a trader to the marrow, more deals could be done, more deals would be done.

Self sufficient now in weapons and food, arms pilfered from battlefield and bunker, food from barn, town and particularly tavern, with souls drenched in the blood of hundreds and vengeance growing cold, the men rested.

Tony set himself next a sentry, where one of their three unused escape routes met the sun, and pondered their future.

The family story spoke of more than one prince who had won his war only to lose the ensuing peace. Fragmented and undependable news from the south, from the wives and children they missed so much, was not all that good.

Safe from imminent bombardment yes, but in an unfamiliar, war-weary city with nought but a child and two old men to watch over them, they did suffer. Not of course as much as Pyotor. This last ambush, manning the machine gun, two fingers and the thumb shot clean off his right hand. Taken from the fight he complained fiercely, father to two dead children, he could still pull a trigger with what was left.

He'd brought his men alive to this point, all of them, Pyotor's wound the worst they had taken, perhaps a sign of changing times. The ambush had been requested by one of the Colonel's grey men. A hoard of looted bullion, best not to reach its intended destination. A trestle was identified, explosives were provided

By some strange mischance of timing, or so it would go if reported, two carriages survived the blast. The second, fortunately, gilt laden.

The first, unfortunately, chock full of battle-hardened armed guards convinced of their Aryan righteousness. A situation not to be taken lightly.

From dark and bulwarked ambush they spat ten minutes of death. None survived, the Russian's wound one in a million.

An omen?

He glanced down the half-choked tunnel to the eighty odd kilos of bullion that had somehow followed them home.

Pyotor's wound would win him release from the war, and a travel warrant to take him far south. His luggage, perhaps war souvenirs. If it proved a little weighty, so what?

The Colonel's men, now heavily indebted to Tony and his band, casually used doors far from Custom's prying eyes. He felt certain, for a percentage, those doors could be his.

He'd met the guardians of many nations' borders. Usually underpaid and mostly neglected many stood sentinel with one eye closed and one hand open. Travelling expenses, the same the world over.

One possible problem.

He cast his eyes back down the tunnel. Thirty feet down in the dim coolness, stripped to the waist, his milk white skin almost shined. The taciturn Scot sent by the British to handle their new explosives.

Resented at first, he'd soon proved his mettle in battle.

Trapped in their box the seasoned guards responded with violent desperation, one lucky shot silenced the Bren gun and defenders gained heart. Then Fergus snatched up the weapon.

Hard on the heels of a high-shrieking war cry, the big bang specialist charged the wood-panelled carriage, shielded by a hail of big calibre bullets.

Some stood to fight, that's where they died, panicked survivors fled into the sharp-eyed rifle fire.

By the time the smoke cleared the band had found a new brother.

But why? But what?

Another British fool eager to die for a far distant, comfortably oblivious Monarch, or a man fighting for his comrades?

Their eyes crossed.

Caught Fergus deep in his own thoughts. He also had a future to consider.

He'd been deep in his powder monkey Da's footsteps on his way down the pit.

Then came the shift when neither his Da, nor those of his friends, came home from the coal face.

Hungry days.

Shifted his attention to the big iron box behind the paymaster's office.

Boom.

Taciturn he would not call himself, cursed himself for the loose-tongued braggadocio in a far valley pub he'd considered a friendly house.

Seven years said the judge.

Then Dunkirk, a panicked British Army and a less than pleasant recruiting lieutenant at the cell door.

Far from the forelock-tugging sycophant Tony feared, the Scotsman proved a man not averse to taking a risk, found himself fond of that brief taste of wealth.

They conversated.

Souvenirs were apportioned, promises made.

Yes, the stars were in line.

Pyotor-led, many hard months later the rest of the band, less one Scotsman, reached their new home. Fergus struggled through de-mob. Released from the army, sentence rescinded for meritorious service, a happy man with cheeks clenched tight and a new life in first class stuck up his arse.

Sometimes smuggling can be simple.

Tony's men meanwhile soaked up the sights and scents of their new home harbour. Their small storm-tossed steam ship, packed near to burst with eager refugees slowed as it slid beneath Sydney's iconic bridge.

A tight-caulked, brightly painted, deck-packed fishing boat with Tony O emblazoned across its prow escorted the weary rust-streaked traveller to its berth at Darling Harbour.

Enjoying her touch, the Englishman stirred, Heather was good with her fingers.

He reached for his temptress.

"Okay okay, prince of a bloke, been telling people what to do for fifty generations, brought his men through the war, didn't get shot, brought home a big box of gold. Does sound like something a prince might do. But a lot of blokes came home unhurt, doesn't make any more unkillable than thousands of others."

He shrugged her further down his thighs, allowed his cock to rise to its demanding height.

She slipped further south, bent and wrapped her lips around its bulbous head. Five or six slow dips while her fingernails danced on the tips of his hips.

Jerry gasped a groan , Heather had been very good with her fingers.

Muscles happily slack, his head dropped back to the pillows.

Heather sat up, swallowed twice to regain her breath and continued.

"That's right, brought his men and all their families safe through a war, brought them half way around the world and bought them all houses when he got here. They are things a prince would do.

And you're right, a lot of blokes came home without holes in them. The war's not the unkillable bit, he didn't get that reputation until he met Nick."

"What?"

"Lay still big guy, want to hear the rest?"

Less distracted now, more interested, he answered slowly.

"Yeah, I do."

"Okay, lie still then, here we go, Tony the unkillable."

"Processed quickly enough, the once savage little band was soon released into the sea of welcoming arms and happily weeping women. Sons saw fathers, for the first time in years wives saw husbands.

Tony stood back, Fulvia in his arms, and saw mouths to feed, lots of them.

One little boat wouldn't do it.

Soon there were two, still not enough.

Charged with selling the catch, Pyotor returned to the four semi-detached cottages Tony had purchased to house his fast-growing clan, husbands and wives were making up for lost time.

He carried some interesting news.

Seems there were soft-bottomed pink skinned men sitting at fish market stalls making more money than the storm-battered sea hunters who brought the haul home.

At sea most of his life, Tony was incensed, with a good ear for an earn, Tony was inspired.

Conversations were conversated, points of view were put. Their resistance proved as hard as their arses, that is, not very.

A new market stall appeared, six more jobs and income improved, enough money now for investment.

Casting canny eyes about, he kept coming back to the swill. That destructive social construct of the times created by wowser politicians and the infant nation's religious tyrants.

They did decree, the pubs shall shut at six.

Created an instant tradition, more evident in Sydney than other towns in this strange giant land still struggling to create its own identity.

North of the harbour, mostly ex-officers and Anglicans, not so bad, south of the harbour, ex-enlisted men, mostly catholic, social terror.

At ten to six a half a million men might front the bars. Four quick schooners, maybe five, to add to the end of the workday's libation, then out the door drunk as a mongrel, The Swill.

Half of them home with thoughts of l'amour.

Half of them home to wives slave to the tenets of their doctrine, obedient to their Sunday pulpit puppet masters, 'NO sex without Babies! Off to Hell with you if you make that man happy!'

From six thirty 'til late bashings and rape abounded.

Driven by this wowsers' law, morally wrong, socially destructive and financially stupid, sly grog shops sprouted like mushrooms.

For the right man, with the right connections, and a crew solid enough to protect his investment, a burgeoning business.

Always the right man, with connections now from the Town Hall to the town drunk, Tony bought one.

One of the best.

His first introduction to the Cross.

Ever been upstairs to the snooker room? Just over the cab rank?

Front of it hasn't changed in thirty years. Up the stairs, left through the door, a counter and a cash register; tea, coffee and soft drinks, a dozen tables with a two-step podium at the end and a half dozen tables for the guys to sit and play cards, and perhaps dissuade uncouth behaviour. A homely kind of place, almost.

Back of the podium a little different now.

That fire door used to lead across the catwalk to another iron door with a trap in it. Knock twice and say the right words, add some money, and your choice of a beer or a flagon would pop straight out. Friendly place.

Down the fire stairs and home for a drink with the poor child-stressed missus."

Heather paused and chuckled in her delivery.

"A social benefactor no less! And if he happened to make a quid on the way, well, he reasoned that was just their Jesus patting him on the back for being a good bloke.

He set a well-padded armchair next to the handrail of the podium steps, scanned his new domain and greeted his new customers as they came through, a head tilt to the buyers, a nod and a wink to the off-duty coppers at play on their permanently reserved corner table.

Dedicated members of their profession, sworn to uphold the rigorous liquor laws of the day, if one of those brown paper bagged bottles of social destruction mysteriously turned up on one of the adjoining tea tables the keen protectors of public order would empty out the contents just as quickly as they could.

Happy men, they somehow seemed to get that opportunity to perform their duties once or twice every game.

He'd bought the place from a fellow refugee, a man who'd chanced the journey decades before, fled the carnage left by the first great war. A man ready for retirement.

Successful in Sydney, the ageing businessman had decided to exchange his hard won assets for five hundred acres of rich Riverina farmland.

Sadly his city-bred sons had other plans. No jumped-up fisherman was taking their inner city cash cow, and neither one was at all interested in the four-legged kind.

'We'll wait until he pays the old man then just run in and shoot him. We're back in business.'

A plan strong on greed and ego but just a little short on research and investment.

The weapon for instance.

An old black powder handgun their father had brought from that long ago war, its charge ageing in the dusty shoe box beneath a forgotten floorboard. Bit of a clean and some new bullets could have done Luigi some good. A little deeper look at Tony's crusty ex-partisan shadow might have helped Gino, maybe saved the old man the extra grief as well.

Anyway, it's his second night in the place. They've come up the stairs and Angie's stopped at the cash register to talk to the manager. He's an old razor gang survivor, scarred old know-it-all came with the place when they bought it. Too in the know to let go.

He and Angie walked around each other a couple of days barring teeth and sniffing arseholes for a couple of days before they both decided it wasn't worth the fight.

Slowly getting to like each other. Named Teddy Fallon."

Jerry stirred.

"Fallon?"

"Yes, Nicky's dad."

"Nicky?"

"That's what Tony calls him, now shut up if you want to hear the rest."

"Yes ma'am!"

"No, that doesn't suit you, now just shut up and listen and let me tell it. Pissing down rainy night, Tony's all suit, jumper, overcoat, layers of protection, all wringing wet, every little bit helps, that's one of his solid beliefs to this very day, makes him pay attention to detail."

"How do you know that?"

She slapped his hardening dick, playfully.

"Settle! 'Cause he told me dopey, now settle. Okay, now, where was I?

Oh yeah, now this is all a fair while back, Nick's about fifteen, mother rotting to death from cancer in the front bedroom, old man drinking himself unconscious every night he's not working, he's moved out of home. Got a job as an apprentice something or other. He's getting paid four fifths of fuck-all, so his old man lets him use the middle table Friday and Saturday nights to pay the rent.

Now you know Nick's not a big guy full grown, when he was a kid he was a skinny little short arse, couldn't reach the long shots so he carried this wire milk crate around the table to stand on.

Made him look silly.

Easier to con the tourist drunks.

Tony, of course, knew the story.

He's walked down the centre of the room, flicked the water off his hat and put it back on his head then gave the boy a quick wink, liked the idea of a young bloke doing his best.

Gave Nick a big lift.

There had been some worry about the new owner. Seemed he was going to be alright after all. He'd reached his chair and turned to sit when the irate brothers burst through the door; surprised the crowd and brought Nick bolt upright. Luigi went right, Gino went left to plunge a six-inch blade into a back turned Sicilian neck.

Luigi's first shot blasted loud and flew straight, Gino turned to join his brother, dreams of swift victory all realised.

Thing about sticking a knife into a Sicilian fisherman, especially one just finished four years of guerilla warfare, you really should make sure he is dead before you turn your back on him.

The blow drove Angie to his knees.

Turned his head painfully to the right to spy the cause of his sudden collapse. A crude wooden handle grew from his thick trap muscle, the point of the blade hard against his collar bone.

He looked hard at the old razor fighter, opened his left palm.

"Gimme."

Teddy jerked the blade free, slapped the bloodied handle into the hard man's hand.

He rose to give chase as Luigi's second shot sounded.

Unlucky boy ,just about to discover he'd killed himself with his first.

Pleased with the new owner, his position in the world secure for the moment, Nick bent to take his shot. Pink off the cushion into the side.

Good shot, happy.

Noise at the front door stood him bolt upright, cue angled across his body.

Hell of a surprise when the timber exploded into splinters three inches from the tip. More shock as the aged round entered his left shoulder and began its journey through his torso.

Through the arm and break the bone, out again and into the chest, four broken ribs and carved a gouge across the sternum, out under the nipple, a breath of fresh air then through the right bicep.

Though stained with his blood and bone, and considerably slowed, the bullet still flew true.

Dead centre at Tony's chest.

Two layers of wet overcoat, woollen jacket and sweater, tie, shirt, singlet, scapular, then buried itself in the breast bone; and stopped.

Spat into his chair like kicked from a horse, Tony gasped painful amazement.

"I'm alive!"

The second shot took his hat.

An angry man doesn't die sitting down, an angry man doesn't die in retreat, he surged to his feet to attack his attacker, took two long steps then slowed, a surprising tableau had appeared.

Nick had spun and flew and bit the carpet.

'You bastard! Killed me! You fucking bastard! I'll kill you fucking back!'

He'd come a cropper a time or two from a motor bike or two so he knew about the moment you use to take stock.

'Start with the legs, yeah, they're still working, arms not so good, wrists move though, specially this right one with the butt of the cue still tight gripped, kinda jammed up against my hip.

Another shot.

'Here comes the murderous fuck right now, running down the aisle, smoke still coming out of the barrel, still pointing it! Forgot me already! Bastard! Watch him now, one stride, two, then a long one right over me. Okay, just tilt the wrist a little, shattered point catch the seam just below the fly.

In!'

The sharp split timber spiked through his testicles and pierced the pelvic floor, then bladder and bowel, momentum and weight driven it kept travelling, through the intestines to separate a vertebrae and finally halt its progress.

Nick gurgled a chuckle.

'Did that hurt?'

Then sank into the black.

Luigi made a strange noise, not a big one, kind of sad for himself now he knew he was dead. By the second shot the citizenry had fled, the last few leaving took a quick look over their shoulders to see the hat fly from Tony's head.

One hour later the news had swept the streets.

'That new snooker room owner, Tony the Dago, dead, one in the heart, one in the head!'

Gino stopped like he'd hit a post. His once hero brother now a silently begging starfish splayed against the table, arms and legs locked rigid with a noxious pool spreading between his feet.

'A boy?'

His thoughts ended as his own blade entered his brain.

Not trusting his damaged right arm to achieve the result required, Angel drove the weapon hammer like with his left, punched the length of the blade clean through the top of his skull. His forensic photos, quite remarkable with a handle on his head, were soon leaked to the press.

His brother's, soon and forever consigned to legend, were not.

Disconcerted coppers rose shakily from the sheltering safety afforded by sturdily built slate tables as Tony circled and juggled possibilities. He massaged a double bloodied bullet in his left hand as he casually discarded facts that didn't suit his needs.

While Teddy knelt to his son Angie motioned for silence, long time campaign comrades he knew his nephew needed a moment to plan.

War had made him quick.

It wouldn't take long.

Two barred doors distant and guarding the grog shop when the first shots rang out, Victor took some time to respond.

The second shot cemented his plan.

'Best make a big entrance, draw the fire, hope the Padrone's not already dead, kill 'em all if he is.'

Hinges flew as the back door crashed open, he launched into the room, 45 calibre automatic souvenirs of his recent Korean service clenched in each fist.

A grand attention grabbing entrance, considerably deflated by Tony's backhand greeting.

'You're late.'

He glanced to the guns, then the unconscious boy.

'Don't need those, he swung his gaze to a quick witted senior sergeant.

Do need a car.'

A set of keys flew across the tables.

'Blue Ford, bottom of the back stairs.'

He didn't know it yet, but Sockeye had just bought himself a pub.

Victor disappeared the colts into custom made underarm slings, quick as a wink, just like they had never been.

Perhaps they hadn't, no one but Tony had seemed to notice them, certainly not the state's stalwart trained observers.

He locked telling eyes with the manager, now hugging his leaking son.

'He's still bleeding, his heart is still beating, not dead!'

To Victor.

'The hospital, quick! If he lives take him home, my bed.'

To the father.

'You, back to work.'

Teddy opened his mouth to protest, his complaint stilled by Tony's next comment.

'He was never here.'

Quick to grasp the sense of removing his already wounded fifteen-year-old son from possible gangland retribution, he swallowed his anger and said something sensible.

'I'll need a new shirt'.

The wounded boss spoke with his eyes. Victor stripped his suave new silk favourite and passed it over, then bent and crushed the boy to his chest, the bleeding slowed.

To Angelo, a red pool spreading beneath his right sleeve.

'You?'

'Good'.

'Well, mister good, you go with him. Get the hole fixed and stay with him. I owe him, we all owe him.'

Victor swept from the room, Angelo close in tow, Teddy buttoned the finest shirt he'd ever owned while Tony gathered the attending police and assisted them with the details they would need to complete their first hand observer reports. Throughout later inquests many would laud the small business owner's willing cooperation with the forces of good. A true pillar of the community.

Some reports seemed to suggest the bullets bounced straight off.

Tony became unkillable."

Story told, Heather slid off her sweaty companion and slipped into the sleep she so badly needed.

Jerry chewed on the tale for ten minutes then allowed his own mind to rest, joined his new found joy in muscle-easing soul healing slumber.

BREAKFAST

PRE-WARNED, AT LEAST AS far as waking him unexpectedly, Denise cracked the bedroom door and paused in the corridor long enough for the dim light and the thick coffee aroma to drift into the single candlelit room. Nick cracked an eyelid, inhaled the day starter's scent and murmured a heartfelt "Ooh, yes please".

He peeled the still sleeping girl's adherent body from his chest and sat up as Denise completed her entrance.

"Thank you. What time?"

"Six, as requested."

"Taxi?"

"Six thirty, just as you asked."

"Bill awake?"

"Michelle's taking her the other half of the coffee pot right now."

"Good. Quick shit and a shower and I'll meet her in the kitchen in twenty. See if you can find her something to wear, black on black with those ball splitter boots no good for a garden breakfast. Lot more use if she's looking good."

The self-possessed working girl answered his demand with a lighthearted rebuff.

"Dopey. Thought you knew something about women. Clothes? We took care of that well before she crashed."

Appropriately chastened for his grumpy bear in the morning manners, not to mention

the obvious mistake, Nick swallowed his coffee and grunted his apology, then rose and headed to the ensuite.

Pleased with her easy victory, Michelle took a good look; remembered nights past and left the room grinning.

Twenty minutes later, Bill, wearing a little yellow summer dress, front buttoned and

short cut, was, of course, looking good.

Except, of course, for the steam boiling out of her ears.

"What time is breakfast?"

"Eight o'clock, early start, he's got people coming."

Never a morning person, Bill had a gripe.

"Then why the fuck am I standing here waiting for a six thirty cab? He sure hasn't moved that castle of his and Darling Point is five minutes away, if that. And what do you mean 'People', what are we? Sheep?"

"Chill girl, no, we're not sheep, but as far as Tony's concerned people means family, everyone else is business, that's us, we're business. And that's why we're up early, business. No point taking food or drink to Tony's table, there's always plenty and you'd probably just insult him anyway.

And that's never clever. Information though, that's always welcome. Now just at the moment I reckon there's some real handy information in some bloke's head out Rose Bay way and I also reckon if you undo the top two buttons on that thing and lean forward just a little, I might not have to punch him to get it."

"Who's the bloke?"

"Won't know until we get there."

"How will you know him?"

"He'll be the lonely guy."

"What?"

"It's complicated girl, just trust me."

While most of the city's wallopers lived comfortably out of Tony's back pocket, as an age old smuggler the water police he flatly refused to pay. A matter of personal principle.

"The seas are free, always have been, always will be."

Consequently his fishing for fun boat frequently copped a legislative once over. Correct flares, good radios, emergency beacons, life vests and, particularly, overloading, they counted heads.

Always a good day out, the boat was usually fully booked.

What with Gino's late entry, Nick figured if he looked, he'd likely find one very unhappy would-be sports fisherman freezing his arse off in a waterside boatshed. Likely left with a bottle of wine, by now likely lamenting his absence from the day's itinerary. With the right interrogator an itinerary likely to be divulged.

Di came through to the kitchen.

"Taxi's outside."

"Thanks, coming now."

They rinsed their cups, house rules, no matter who you were, then up the hall, a half step stop for Nick to collect the bag on loan from Tom and Jerry, felt the bling rattle round in the little space inside, then out to the car.

Doors closed, directions given then off to the east.

Just off the main road, a weather beaten blue boatshed, a light on inside.

Nick leaned over the seat back and unfastened the top two buttons of Bill's bodice, almost caused an accident through the driver's mirror, and pointed to the high heels held in her left hand.

"Put those on, he'll likely be half drunk by now, give him both barrels, they do make your arse look good."

He ducked the left hand slap response and continued his instructions.

"Right, now you're here for Gino, don't want to hang around waiting, where has he gone and when will he be back? There's a heap of shoals they fish off out there, could spend days looking for them."

Bill headed to her unsuspecting quarry, Nick handed the driver a cigarette, stepped out to share a smoke and wait for events to unfold. Not long.

Bill stepped back to the cab. Heels in her left hand, shaking her right.

"What happened?"

"They're some reef about thirty miles out, East south east."

Nick nodded, smiled in thanks, he knew the spot, turned his eyes to her right hand.

"What happened?"

"Rude little prick, Insisted I stay and wait with him."

Cab driver's eyes went to the sky, not an idiot.

Nick swallowed a grin, he had an idea of what came next, just wanted to be sure, just for fun.

"Not interested?"

"Shit Nick, I got my standards, with a nose that broke he's too damn ugly and with nuts that crushed he'd be useless anyway."

The now buttoned-up Bill sank her buttocks to the back seat and demurely swung her legs aboard.

"Can we go now?"

"Yes we can go now."

The driver turned his head, widened his eyes to ask a destination.

"Back to Heather's, then Tony's back gate."

"Back gate, what are we, plumbers?"

"Jesus girl, what's up your arse this morning? You wake up looking for a fight? No, we're not plumbers. The front door is for everybody, telephone salesmen, Jehovah's Witnesses, invited guests. They get as far as the front parlour, back gate gets you access all areas, shouldn't be hard to understand, most clubs work the same way."

Bill settled for the ten minute ride.

They pulled to the kerb, the tree dappled street, all morning sunshine, nothing to see here. Sharp sounds, even shots, in the middle of the Cross, in the middle of the night, were often ignored. Heather, as always, on time and set to go, stepped from the gate in a light linen suit, wrapped in a cloud of happy.

Nick stepped from the cab, opened the back door and asked a cheeky question. Just to make sure. "Second half of last night get any better for you?"

Heather smiled a hidden smile, replied. "Just a little."

"Give me a minute, need to talk to him."

Heather questioned with her eyes while she passed him the keys to let himself in.

"All good, just need him to collect something for me."

Jerry drifted from dreamy reminisce to sharp-eared wakefulness as Nick trod up the stairs.

"Thought you were going to breakfast."

"Good morning to you too. And yes, I am."

"So why have I gotta be awake?"

"Need you to do something for me, take a run out to Glebe."

"Glebe?"

"Need a boat."

"Mama's pissed, you haven't been there for months, starting to think you don't like 'em anymore."

"How do you know that?"

"You're kidding. You know how good the food is. I eat there at least once a week. How come you don't? And they never let you pay."

"You get a welcome when you go there?"

"Yeah, always."

"Me too, gets a bit embarrassing, now even the kids start yelling when I walk in."

"So what? Suck it up, you still gotta go see her."

"Yeah, yeah, I know, just not today. Need you to meet me down Jesus dock."

"When?"

"10.30am."

The tall pommie rolled from the bed and stepped towards the shower.

"You seem pretty certain, you called 'em yet?"

"No, but, you know she's pissed just from me missing some meals, how she going to be if I ask someone else for a boat ride. Love 'em all to death but she is just evil jealous."

"Yeah, there is that. See you there."

Jerry ran hot water on his head, Nick stepped back to the cab. Found the girls in quiet back seat discussion, something sad about Robyn and girls at the Apple. Looked to Nick like girls' club business. He kept his head out of that.

The driver needed no direction to Tony's front door. Broad, sweet-scented avenue with branches arching over the roadway, stone wall and grandiose front gate. They drove straight past, Nick pointed, the narrow lane, fifty metres down and turn left. The spiked steel barriers slid sideways as they pulled to a halt. Pyotor took his hand off the button and waved them across to his gatehouse, the comfortable, deep verandahed stone cottage he called home. The one with the wine press and cool, well-stocked cellar. With the neat little work shop and well-stocked armoury.

With the pitch of the road and the waist-high stone balustrade the newly arriving trio didn't spy Pyotor's earlier guests until they reached the four stone steps. Nick had noticed the quiet mirth in Pyotor's eyes, a joke? A trick? What? Now he saw it reflected in the eyes of Victor the Viking, last night's invisible man. A young stranger stood with him. A dark-haired well shaped young man, wearing blue corduroy trousers and an unusual style of boots.

The source of their mirth stood exposed.

They were waiting for Nick to question Vic of his lack of appearance.

Nick shook Pyotor's three fingered hand with comfort, something he'd been doing most of his life, while introductions were made. Bill first, of course to Pyotor. The old watchman smiled, still appreciated the sight of a fine young woman on a warm summer morning.

Then Victor spoke up.

"Tarik. My sister's husband's cousin's nephew."

Nick shook his hand and replied.

"Ah, the young man in the tree, good to meet you."

He watched the mirth fade from their eyes, quickly replaced by wonder.

In truth, he had been concerned for his friend's no show. Right up to the point, in a brief flash of light, he had spotted the edge of a unique gun case, blue corduroy pants and paratroop boots clutching the bough of a tree. Victor had been up higher, with that night sighted and silenced 222.

He turned to the recently hidden sniper.

"You know you could have saved some trouble if you put one in Gino last night."

Victor recovered quickly, replied with a grin and a private joke.

"Dead man on the street, come on Nick, you know how hard it is to get rid of a body nowadays." Their history had been long and sometimes exciting. The girls stood confused for a moment, while explanations ensued Nick opened the satchel to show the short cut guns and inquire of the old armourer.

"Got any salt loads for these things?"

"Salt?"

"Yeah mate, if these things really do have to go off today there could be a crowd, and most of 'em don't deserve to be shot. Salt will do the job with no one dying."

"They'll be ready after you see the old man."

"Don't know if I am looking forward to that, he must be pissed off this morning."

"Angry? Yes, a little bit, but sad, very sad."

"Why sad? His grandson's coming of age, friends and family all around. Family is everything to him, why sad?"

"They are his children, and he must now split them apart."

He stepped from the company of friends into the broad cool of the cottage, drifted just far enough for the next question to remain unheard, he suspected what it would be, the great sin, the great secret kept by just four.

Nick spoke it quietly.

"Does he know?"

"No, not that, if he did he wouldn't push them apart, he'd just tear the boy to shreds. Fulvia's right, he can't ever know, that would kill him, probably is what started it though."

One night, in a rare moment of drunkenness, Fulvia had spilled it. She had been sad, Nick and Pyotor had gently probed. They broke her.

At sixteen he'd decided he was all grown up, no need any more to obey this bossy big sister. He'd show her. Fuck her! Yeah that's what he'd do. Grab her by the throat, bend her over the bench and fuck her in the arse. That would show the domineering bitch!

He tried.

They later agreed to tell their father the injuries sustained came from falling off his new motorcycle.

Pyotor's offhand comment hit Nick in the face like a bucket of water, woke him to the obvious.

Brian had been very wrong, he had considered himself young Tony's target, his end game.

Not so.

He had been right in one way. He'd called young Tony's machinations war; in that he had been right, but not a small war, not an argument between innkeepers for pride of the street. A big war, a war of succession, a war between siblings for pride of the city. A clash of ego and philosophy to affect the city for decades to come.

Tony loved cocaine. Tony liked obedient mistresses, Tony liked his dick, Tony liked to see fear in people's eyes. He'd practised hard to become an arsehole. Fulvia loved her family. As her father's paymaster she had long known the power of the law, had learnt how money paid to men in blue suits or funny wigs caused problems to disappear. She had studied hard for her own funny wig.

Only a fool would support the boy, or someone with no idea.

For fools he had Frankie and Gino.

For the dirty work he reached out to people with no idea. The new wave. The new tide of humanity wracked by wayward princes, priests and politicians. Homes and lives destroyed, generational communities shattered by shot and cannon fire. Angry, confused, shell shocked young men, perfect for would-be gangsters.

No thought, of course, these young men also had families, Nick somehow felt that would come back on him one day.

He stepped back on the porch and asked Victor, "You coming up for breakfast?"

The answer surprised him.

"No, not yet, I'll be back for the birthday cake, gotta take a drive out to Hurlstone Park first."

"Where? Tony know you're going out west today?"

Victor smiled a happy smile.

"Tony knows, he's sending me, the boy's about to find out."

The big man plucked a set of keys from the rack, stepped across the gravel drive to warm a comfortable car.

Nick gathered up the girls and their new-found companion, stepped down the steps and turned towards the discreet breakfast garden. As they rounded the south side of the big old stone house, the long rectory table came slowly to view. Some sights Nick had expected, Tony at the head, in his familiar chair, Angelo to his right, Fulvia to his left, other sights he found surprising.

The table for one usually overcome with generosity now almost bare, coffee cups for each and a squat aged urn set in the centre, steaming slowly, and what is that? A framed photograph? No, something older, a small portrait painting, then the guests.

While two were familiar, the son and the son in law Tony and Frank, Nick had not expected them at this table. The others, to Nick, were brand new. Older men, bearded, in robes and skull caps. Their eyes followed him.

Many of the conversations at Tony's tables were conducted in silence, especially the important ones.

While her guest's eyes were occupied, Fulvia spoke to Heather. Swept her glance across the bearded men, tightened her lips and looked to the chairs set that end of the table, Heather took the message, took Bill by the hand and sat down.

Tarik, clever man, read the signs and took the seat next to them, watched close as the conversation continued.

Tony rose to take Nick's outstretched hand, still impressive with his height but no longer the bulk of the broad thick chest, Tony was ageing fast.

Nick could see the years in him, saw some had been harder than others.

While they shook, Nick took a shock.

The bearded guy nearest him opened his mouth and stated out loud the secret kept quiet for so long.

"The boy who shared your bullet."

To his greater surprise Tony responded.

"Yes, and much more."

And then the stunner.

"It never ends."

Words unbidden rose reflexively to his throat.

"It never changes."

Tony's old adage he suddenly realised had a lot more history to it than he had supposed.

"Who were these guys?" He asked himself.

For a long moment Tony allowed himself the pleasure of Nick's rare confusion. A lonely bright start in a dark morning. He blamed himself, what should have been a day of celebration, his grandson's manhood, his daughter raised to arcane fraternity of those who owned the law, even the re-emergence of a lost branch of the bloodline, all overshadowed by the dark cloud he'd ignored for far too long. He should have whipped the boy years ago. Basta! Enough!

He dragged himself from his growing gloom, reached to the table and lifted the small portrait. Two men, bearded, bandaged. Archaic clothes, swords even, a small table between them with a squat coffee urn set up on it.

Nick somehow felt certain the urn on that table and the one on Tony's were one and the same.

Tony explained.

First by introducing the stranger who'd spoken "Abdul Raffic, my cousin."

Next his silent companion.

"Abdul Haqq. You must excuse Abdul Haqq, he speaks no English."

From the flash of eyes and the shift of posture as they spoke, Nick knew that to be untrue. He figured Tony knew it too. To be expected, a common play, useful for private conversation in the midst of public debate. They exchanged words in some form of Arabic. Then pointed to the portrait.

"Our grandfathers, partners in business, wounded together at Sevastopol, both by the same French cannon. And more, there were women, there were children, we have new family to welcome."

Nick shared smiles and greetings, took a seat next to the girls.

Tony continued.

"Today should be a happy day, but there is one sad problem, perhaps you could help."

"How can we help?"

"Two of their young men came to town last night, to do some things for my son's man Gino. Now they are hurt, one may not walk again."

"Not my man! He left!"

He absorbed his son's outburst as best he could, turned to Nick and continued.

"Yes, he left. But where did he go. This is our problem. Do you think you can help?"

Nick smiled in return, pointed a question at Tony and Frank.

"Gino? Big guy, black hair, real arsehole? That Gino?"

Their answer, eager in unison, if not so transparent almost funny to watch.

"Yeah, yeah him!"

Happy to shed any call on last night's debacle, Nick turned back to Tony and his bearded visitors.

"Well he's a big loud bastard, shouldn't be hard to find. Reckon I could do that today."

Abdul Haqq questioned his companion, Tarik translated.

"Today?"

"Yes, today, good chance. Be happy to let you know how it goes."

"That would be good news."

From the panic in his voice and the cringe of his shoulders Tony saw his son's fear, from his words he heard his attempt to shift blame to a lackey. He failed all tests himself, denied any hope of leadership. Tony smoothly took the burden of guilt, began to make some changes.

"And what did this man do for us before last week?"

Tony jumped to answer, he'd heard the 'us' in his father's words, thought himself freed of consequences.

"Cars, he ran the showroom out of Hurlstone Park."

That large legitimate car yard, so necessary to cover their cut and shunt thefts.

"That is a valuable business, have you been there to see how he left it?"

The brothers in law saw a hope to escape the uncomfortable table. They swapped glances and answered in tandem.

"We were going out there today."

Their eagerness shone a light on their guilt.

Tony turned slightly to engage Abdul Raff, murmured quietly.

"It never ends."

The siblings in marriage heard the gentle words, had no idea what they meant. Raffi raised a finger in silent acceptance, he knew their guilt, accepted his cousin's impending judgement.

"Good idea, but not you Frank, not today. Mario's day, he sleeps now, you should be here when he wakes, Tony can go, tomorrow you can join him. That's a big yard, will take the two of you to run it."

Tony's stomach turned, angry bile rose to his throat, for the first time in his life he made a clever decision, he swallowed it. The succession had been settled, not in his favour. Sat silent, his father addressed him again.

"Another thing, small but important. When our cousins came to visit they travelled by taxi. This is unfitting, and we have many fine cars. Victor will drive you all out there, while you're busy he can help them choose suitable vehicles."

The deal had been done, gifts exchanged, the refugee clan had two fine new cars, Tony had an old coffee pot, a faded pictrograph and a brand new ally in the west. Both camps would be well satisfied, as soon of course as the Gino problem had been solved.

Victor, of course, had been listening, emerged round the edge of the hedge right on cue.

"Aah, your transport is ready."

Tony farewelled his guests and their fellow traveller, the new car yard boss, then spoke to his son in law.

"Frank, you look like shit. Look like you been up all night. Mario won't be up for an hour or two, you should get some rest."

He took his dismissal in silence, he knew he'd dodged a bullet.

Tony sat to address the crew.

"Where is he?"

Nick answered with a smile.

"Gone fishing."

Tony stood nonplussed for a moment, then realised just what Nick meant. He smiled wide and queried, just to make sure.

"With Tomas?"

"Yes."

"He's trapped."

"Yes, just got to go get him."

Tony sunk into silence and gave it some thought.

"There will be many eyes."

"That's the trick, get him off the boat."

"How?"

"With help."

"What do you need?"

Nick turned to Angelo.

"That radio still working?"

Angelo replied with a nasty grin. He liked hunting.

"Yes."

"Well that, a bikini for Bill, a loud car for Heather so people will notice, and another body to fill a seat, someone who can fight a bit would be good, just in case."

Tony smiled, he had his own small surprise.

"Car is easy, Fulvia has more swim suits than David Jones and I have just the body, I'm told he can fight a bit too."

He raised his voice just a little.

"Lionel."

Last seen disappearing in the dark, all dressed in black, with an unconscious young man over one shoulder, the orphan kiwi presented his made over appearance. New polo shirt, tan slacks and a comfortable pair of leather loafers.

He'd taken a call at the game before Nick's arrival.

"Keep an eye on the birthday boy."

They'd met months before, when Fulvia had brought him to the game. Liked the look of each other straight away. He'd used his own initiative, used that thing he used best, delivered on the run, the six foot South Auckland right hand.

Delivered just right, hard enough to turn the lights out not so hard to break bones. Timeing just right, behind a bright flash of light, all unseen, no need to trouble their growing friendship.

Tony explained.

"Lionel's going to work here now. Mario and Tarik can run the club, he will drive and keep an eye."

"That will leave a hole in the game."

"The bookkeeper."

"Dave?"

"Do him good, he mixes with too many children. Is that all you need?"

"That's all for today, but there is one thing I'd like to talk to you about."

"What's that?"

"I'm leaving."

The reply surprised everyone, even Fulvia, whose mouth the word came from.

"Don't."

Eyes turned her way, she took a quick thought and she continued.

"Tony's gone west, that loud-mouth bitch in the house can go with him. We need someone to live there."

The excuse was thin, but it did cause Nick to waver. Tony caught the mood.

"Of course you couldn't live there now."

Just a small sneer appeared in his voice.

"She has decorated."

He jumped one thought to another.

"I hear you like Queensland."

Nick took a turn at quick thought. Of course someone had spoken. Tony, as always, two steps ahead of the game.

Tony continued.

"I have a friend. He has a place up there, very nice. You might know it, Ellis Beach."

Nick knew it. That little slice of paradise half way between Cairns and Port Douglas. A well-stocked bar, a well-scented kitchen, a dozen cabins, palm trees and a beachfront twenty feet distant.

"Perhaps, after today, you could visit. Stay a couple of weeks, give us time to do the house."

"Sounds bloody nice, but mate, I am getting tired of this Tarantino movie."

"What about this, two years, just until the boys get the hang of things. Lionel can guard them, Heather can watch the business but it would be good if they had your advice."

Sounds okay but that will leave a hole at Feathers."

Tony turned straight onto Bill.

"You, young lady. What do you think of girls who work for a living?"

Bill threw it straight back.

"If a girl makes that choice she deserves every penny she can earn. If someone else makes that choice for her that someone deserves to be dead."

Tony smiled at Nick.

"Seems Heather has a replacement to teach."

While Fulvia took Bill to the poolside change room, a range of bikinis to explore, Nick gathered the troops and laid out the plan. When she returned, with a towel around her shoulders, they rose and bid their adieu.

Gone fishing

HE LEANT AGAINST THE guardrail of the short public dock, checked the time and began to worry, just a little bit.

"Jesus, where the fuck are they?"

Since their IT business took off the boys, understandably, had allowed their attention to the sick boat business to grow a little slack. They'd kept the latest boat in survey but Cong would not let them put it in the water until both outboards had been serviced, electrics all proved and safety gear stowed. Jerry'd pretended to be in a hurry while he sat there and ate like a king. Didn't fool Mama Sam, she just stood there and kept passing him small bowls of delicious things while she wheeled the latest gossip from his soy- soaked lips.

Nick chuckled despite himself. Unbidden memory, the night the dock revealed its hidden secret and earned its name.

Rushcutter's Bay, Nick's early teenage playground. The boys in the gang had discovered that many of these luxurious yachts moored in the bay held bars, fridges and freezers, all well stocked. Borrowing a row boat, at night, was never difficult. A night on the piss, for free! Discovered strange new things like Moet Chardon, boy didn't that girlie fizz get you pissed! Then back in the boat and back to the dock, arms laden with frozen steaks, pre-cooked pastas and bottles yet undrunk. Food for a fortnight, the row boat owner could find it tied in the morning.

That mistake taught Nick about planning escapes. Highly unimpressed yacht owners, of the wealthy kind, contacted Sydney police, of the senior kind. Complaints from the city's elite of course bought massive response.

Pride of the fleet, the biggest, fastest newest pursuit boat on the harbour, moored in the ambush across the bay, hidden in the shadows of Potts Point's height.

Fortunately for the boys, hubris played its usual hand, they should have brought a smaller boat. Slipping under the anchor chains, darting from yacht to yacht while the big cruiser made its turns, the boys worked their way back towards the jetty. Then the last bit, thirty metres of open water to the harbour wall, nine feet high at low tide, tall slick and unscaleable, one hundred metres to the dock. They braved it as best they could, but it wasn't going to work.

The big boat made its turn.

Ten feet from the wall, thirty metres from the dock Dennis told everyone.

"Fuck this, I'm swimming!"

For the men who built the wall, so long ago, some with chains still on their feet, this wasn't the first. They knew full well how the sea undercut so foundations were built deep and wide. Dennis had found them. One a moonless night one inch below the surface.

By the time his left foot hit the water he was sprinting. One surprised roar rang from a dozen throats.

"Jesus!"

The boys soon followed their new found messiah. Lots of hysterical laughter. Sadly, that was the end of free champagne.

He was still smiling as the fast boat's twin wakes coursed the curve of the point, Hai Trang at the wheel, brother Ba as always at his elbow and Jerry, propped amidships and grinning like a loon, beautiful day on Sydney Harbour.

Jerry threw a line, Bill caught it and tied it to a cleat as the brothers stormed ashore.

"Phuck Nick!"

"Phuck Nick!"

Bill bent her knees, Tarik slid his right foot back and clenched his fists. Lionel and Jerry now saw it and burst into laughter.

As the brothers swarmed Nick with handshakes, hugs and bright big grins, Tarik and Bill stood confused. Bill asked.

"What's this, fuck you, then a handshake?"

Nick replied.

"Not fuck, phuck. Means good luck, blessings."

"Fuck Nick means good luck? That's something new."

"No mate, that's Vietnamese, and its phuck with a P H not an F."

"Where the fuck did that idea come from?"

It was an old story, Jerry and Lionel had heard it more than once, didn't mind hearing it again, had a good ending, bad things for bad guys. Nick pointed to the eight seater fast boat.

"Get in, tell you on the way."

Started out, one night Nick went to talk to a man about a dog. A common expression, it usually meant 'I am going to talk to someone about something that's none of your business'. This time it meant dog.

Nick had a mate named Harry, Harry had a dog named Bruce, a racing dog, a greyhound, Bruce ran real fast.

Another bloke, who lived over near the dog track in Glebe, also had a dog, a racing dog, one that didn't run as fast as Bruce.

Nasty fella, snuck into the kennels one night and changed Bruce's racing career with a stick. No proof of course, but everyone in the know did know.

Nick liked dogs, Nick liked Harry, had a free night on his hands so decided on a trip to Glebe and a conversation with a dog trainer. Turned out the bloke was a strong and boisterous debater, Nick discovered he had to break several of his strong points before he was willing to lay down quietly and admit the error of his ways.

Time to leave.

The debate had proven a little louder than Nick had hoped, neighbours' comments could be heard, comments like "Call the Police." A hasty back door exit was looking good, looked a lot better when he spotted the helmet, gloves and keys on the back door table.

"Gotta be a bike here somewhere."

He pulled back the tarp in the dark corner of the yard and blessed his lucky stars. The very best inner city getaway vehicle ever built. The Kawasaki three-cylinder,

500cc, two stroke, you could ride it, if it didn't kill you. Some maniac design engineer back at the factory swapped the throttle for a trigger, gave it a power band about as wide as a human hair. All or nothing. Damn hard to keep the front wheel on the ground. Nick decided to ride uphill. He was still feeling pumped from the hearty debate so he chose a particular hill that he and Pete discovered back in their motocross days, Beattie Street. Very steep street. If you timed it just right, wait at the bottom for the red light on top, count ten then hit it. If you reached the intersection at anything over sixty miles per hour there was no need to put your tyres on Glebe Point Road at all. If you arrived doing over seventy you could cross the far side six feet in the car.

Quick bike, Nick went for height. Bad luck the rear foot peg was just right to clip the young copper just behind the ear. Nick had seen him too late, already out of the car, no time for anything but prayer.

Funny just how and when life can throw you a lesson. Nick learnt something of relativity, how time could stretch. Within that fractured micro second of panic he accomplished a great deal.

Reacquainted himself with that long-forgotten God of his catholic days, offered up a small entreaty, remembered that long long weekend under Darlinghurst cells learning the folly of punching a policeman, no charges of course, just rotating shifts of cranky young coppers explaining the point.

Deciding he would hate to discover the consequences of bashing one over the head with a motorbike.

Remembered the rear foot peg was a spring loaded fold up peg, not a solid man killing bar, thanked his old/ new deity for the small miracle, asked for another as he planned his escape. There were certain to be two coppers in the car so the call would go out immediately, all access to the peninsular suburb would be closed in minutes. Don't run, hide, ditch the bike, hat and gloves, take a walk, take a cab.

But where?

There was a lane, a bent one, with garbage bins and shadows.

He took a left, then another, saw the dark slit in the wall and slid in.

Bike behind a bin, hat and gloves on the seat, keys in ignition, bit of luck someone might steal it. Nick squeezed into that narrow block of shadow, face knees and feet pressed against the paling fence at ground level as the police beam sliced the darkness. Missed him.

"Fuck, that was quick, they must be cranky."

Nick's sphincter began to relax, five more minutes in the shadows then gently to feet and a walk down the street. That was the plan.

That was when An screamed, six feet away, just over the fence.

The gap in the palings Nick shifted slightly caught half the tableau. Two bald guys had hold of a little fella, were starting to punch him. Another scream, cut short. Nick shifted again, caught the other half of the picture. The other skinhead had hold of a tiny woman, one hand held her head and closed her mouth, the other held the remains of her skinny torn dress.

"You bastard! So much for a quiet stroll home!"

One foot on a bin, one foot on the top of the fence and launch.

Flying scissor front kick, wrapped in Johnny Reb boots. A very loud 'Fuck!' from an unseen upstairs window, the young sons had been learning English.

The would-be rapist spotted him coming, opened his mouth in alarm. Nick's right boot fit in pretty well. Especially when the jaw broke and all those loose teeth got out of the way. He fell down.

Thug number two released his hold on the little guy, turned to confront Nick, then something unexpected. With one side released, the little guy spun, rolled a long arm through the air. His victim yelled and dropped, the elbow pointing down, the hand pointing up. That did look painful. The surprise slowed number two just long enough for Nick to catch him with a hard right hand, smash his nose, gushed ample evidence of violent confrontation down the front of his shirt drove him back to the fence. More yelling, this time from behind, An Trang, behind a hastily donned apron, burst through the back door, a bloody big meat clever in her hands, two young boys and a tiny girl behind her, all with knives in their fists.

Broken nose displayed his athleticism, hardly touched the top of the fence, and look at this! A bike! Helmet for disguise and keys in the lock!

"So long suckers! I'll be back!"

Nick burst into laughter as the bike roared off, dragged the two damaged shitheads to their feet and pushed them out the gate. Pushed them to the right, their mate wouldn't get far, didn't want them to stumble into his interrogation.

Cong Trang gathered his small brood and stared at Nick quizzically.

"Phuck. This bad, why you laugh?"

"No mate, this would have been bad but I figure I did you a favour, so why the fuck do you keep swearing at me?"

Confusion reigned for a moment, until elder son Han explained his surprise when Nick flew through the air out of the dark. Explained, in Vietnamese to his father that, in English, fuck was a word which expressed surprise.

To Cong, it made sense, he turned to Nick to clear the air, to explain that, in Vietnamese Phuck meant good luck and blessings.

It all fitted.

Nick extended a handshake, "My name's Nick".

It all made sense. Out of the night, great blessings.

Cong shook the extended hand.

"Yes, yes, fuck Phuck Nick."

Nick almost objected, then the aroma from the open back door hit his nostrils. Mouth instantly to water, stomach screaming 'you haven't fed me!'

An caught his hesitation, she knew about her own cooking. Took him meekly by the hand and led him indoors.

"Come, eat, tell us why you laugh."

They ate and spoke through the rest of the night,

Nick told them the events that brought him to their home.

Cong told him of the little restaurant just south of Saigon, where they learnt some rough English from Australians and Yanks. Then the defeat and arrival of the battle-scarred Communist overlords. Two families and the bamboo raft pushed through the waves.

The boys spoke. Spoke of pride and fear. Pride in their father and his brother Han. Each over the side in turn to scrape algae from the underside, to net scarce fingerlings to feed to the wok. On the last dry metre of deck, that tiny flickering flame fed with thin slivers of bamboo and precious scrapes of coal, at night that tiny primordial altar surrounded by fearful faces. Their father's voice, softly spoken through the night, giving hope, holding back the despair, denying the hunger that gnawed their bellies.

An spoke, spoke of heartache. Close to the water, the horizon quite near. The Australian patrol boat was almost upon them, all heads turned. Nobody saw the shark. A swirl, a splash, blood in the water, Han gone. Tragedy and salvation all in two breaths. Yin met Yang as merciless as fate might be. They spoke of the future, of aspirations and education.

Two policemen came by.

Just to check a bruised thing's unlikely story. Innocently attacked while taking a piss in a lane, by a man who could fly and his gang of mad knife-wielding midgets. They'd already been to the stolen bike's address. Called the owner an ambulance. His description of his attacker wasn't quite right but he had obviously been struck about the head several times, a discrepancy easily ignored.

"Was he here?"

The smiling An replied.

"No, no, all good, Australia good, happy happy. Here, have some dumplings." The sergeant took a bite as the car rolled away.

"How fucking good are these things!"

The policemen returned often, every shift in fact and what a surprise, they paid! And so did everyone else. The family would survive, but education was expensive.

The boys worked that one out for themselves.

Friday and Saturday nights they packed take away for early morning fishing clubs.

The most common and quite frequent complaint they heard was of one or two sea sick customers in the boat, ruined everyone's day. At a hundred bucks a head for the day's fishing they figured another ten per head to rid themselves of the green tinged party poopers would seem quite reasonable. They needed a boat. A quick one. The first one was made of wood, with a Holden motor amidships. Nick came for the test drive. Iron motor smashed its way through wooden keel about five hundred metres off North Bondi. They straggled ashore not real happy. The next boat had a metal hull, and outboards. An eight seater proved just right. Four trips per weekend, minus expenses made two grand per week. Easily enough for their education plus money to bring lost relatives south.

The latest boat now sported twin hundred horses, a very quick boat.

They cleared the point of Rushcutter's Bay and turned the boats nose east.

While the engines gurgled back into life Han asked the obvious.

"Where are we going?"

"Watson's Bay Pub."

"What? Thought they were in a hurry?"

Ba threw a glance Jerry's way. Nowadays an IT success, they'd been roused early and worked hard.

"We are mate, but, ever hear how haste makes waste? Gotta take care of the details along the way. There's going to be someone disappear today. True, he's a shithead but every chance his mother still loves him, someone might ask. Best seen back on land by a lot of people. Someone seen picking him up would be good.

"How you going to do that? Magic?"

"Yes mate. Well almost. Call it illusion, tell me Jerr, you feeling supple?"

"Why?"

The reply surprised Nick, he expected a definite yes. Seeing how the giant ninja's favourite means of entry was to fold himself into a box and have himself delivered.

"Well mate, what I want is for a lot of people to see six go out and seven come back, it is only just opening time but seeing the Watto is the most beautiful pub in the world, I expect at least a hundred people to see us."

Tarik interrupted.

"Is this the pub of daughters?"

"Yes mate."

That bought Bill's ever-protective head up.

"What daughters?"

They had five miles of water to cross, easily time for explanation. The pub had been built in the Forties, to service the navy base top of the headland.

"No particular daughters, just advice friendly old salts give to young sailors coming through, kind of like Officer and Gentlemen, but in reverse."

"Oh yeah, and what's that?"

"Goes something like this. If you're ever having a drink, with a pretty girl in the garden of the Watson's Bay Hotel and she says 'Oh look, you can see my house from here', you marry that bitch because her daddy's rich". Bill frowned, not sure how to take it.

The boys cracked up. Thought it good advice.

"Now, can we go back to business."

He turned back to Jerry, motioned to the cable locker, reckon you can fit in there for ten minutes?

A short cut short of laughter from Hai and Ba left Nick confused until Jerry lifted his shirt to display an unusually distorted stomach.

"No chance mate, I've been eating for an hour."

"Okay then, plan B. How about we drop you round Camp Cove for fifteen minutes." He pointed to the bloated stomach.

"Reckon you can bob around for fifteen minutes without sinking?"

"No worries mate." He patted his belly. "Rice wontons and prawns, Mama cooks light, they float."

A little bit of laughter through the boat.

Nick tapped Hai on the shoulder.

"Camp Cove, go wide round the point, keep us out of sight until we get to the pub."

Camp Cove, when God finished building Australia she was mighty pleased with her handiwork, so pleased in fact she decided to put a cherry on top. Reached down to that secluded, pristine Aegean cove, plucked it up and tucked it in just behind South Head. Tumbledown hill to the east, rock-strewn, tree studded and green fringed, the beach a fifty metre spread of glistening white, a light forest park dressed the point to the west. With the narrow path around the point meandering and indistinct, most visitors arrived by boat. Three there now, all moored together, allowed crews and guests to mingle, swap stories and drinks, cocaine and bodily fluids.

Jerry slid over the transom, turned on his back and slow kicked away.

"You alright for fifteen?"

He smiled in return, face just above the water, he soaked in the sights and the scents, oh what a way to spend a day!

The crew hurried back to the pub.

Nick gave direction as they neared the beach.

He tapped the brothers' shoulders.

"We won't be long, you two may as well stay here."

To Lionel and Tarik.

"Over the other side of the park there's a little chemist come tourist shop, need a sun hat, one of them straw things with a brim."

Lional queried.

"A hat? What for?"

"Don't know the prick all that well but I do know he's got a big head covered in black hair, Jerry's got a big bald dome. What's the best way of hiding that?"

"A hat."

They headed across the park.

He turned to Bill.

"Come on girl, shirt off, tits out, we want to be seen, we go buy some beer."

All back in the boat in ten, scooped a happy man from the water on their way to the heads.

From the moment the big shithead stepped aboard, Tomas knew something was wrong, wasn't hard to pick. While the rest of the group dressed in old fishing gear, Gino'd arrived in his nightclub finery. Silk shirt, bright black and red leather jacket and fine leather dancing shoes. Thing that really gave him away was the butt of a handgun under his armpit.

Tomas watched.

When they reached the shores Gino'd pulled off the jacket, moved to the prow and pulled out the cannon.

To Tomas it now made sense.

The gun had been naughty and now it had to go swimming, nothing unusual there. Gino held the thing in his hands, felt its weight and admired its ugly beauty. Good gun. He thought.

"Fuck 'em!"

He'd began to grow courage when the boys in the boat shed had wilted under its threat. Shaking hands had tended the small hole in his right bicep while he held the thing in his left, gritted his teeth and swore, just to show them how tough he was.

"My gun, and I'll shoot anyone who doesn't like it!"

He stuck the weapon back in its sling, grinned like a loon and sat with his back to the wheelhouse.

Tomas began to worry. No matter where, no matter when, some things never change. When a gun has to go swimming, it has to go swimming. This moron had changed his mind. A lunatic on a boat with a loaded weapon is never a good thing. Without the jacket the rough bandaged wound stood right out. Worser and worser.

The old skipper's heart jumped a beat when the white noise on the ship-to-shore radio missed a dot, returned and missed a dash. Angelo!

Threw him back to the days of a strapping young partisan. Strong enough to carry not only his rifle, ammo and grenades but also the cumbersome Australian Army issue morse code set. For weeks on end, on Tony's orders, they'd sat around the fires at night and spoke to each other in dots and dashes. Kept it up until all in the troop spoke the language with ease. An imbedded memory. He lifted the handpiece from the radio console, pressed the send button twice to acknowledge, then listened close. Discovered a couple of things. The good news, cavalry on the way, the bad news, his engines would soon suffer fuel problems. With just a small adjustment to the full air mix he made the second come true. For a full half hour, while the motors coughed and spat, the crowded boat pitched in the swell. Tomas kept an eye on Gino, watched his head go red and steam appear at his ears, he was getting cranky with their slow progress. One eye out for the cavalry.

Twin wakes! Just over there! Not horseman but a fast little boat!

Tomas eyed the oncoming vessel with relaxed curiosity, Gino with suspicion, he crouched behind the wheelhouse grasping the weapon.

As they slowed and neared Ba stood and called to Tomas.

"Hey skipper do you have one for us?"

Tomas knew the brothers, over the years they had taken dozens of his suffering sailors back to the hard. Lately though, very conspicuous in their absence. They had been missed. Their sudden reappearance suggested he might be rid of the obnoxious fool. He played along. Turned to his passengers.

"It's the seasick boat."

Hai added his line.

"Room for one more."

With suspicions sinking Gino stood taller, took a better look. Had his ego allowed he'd have cursed himself for cowardice. He saw a couple of weak-arsed midget slopes, half a dozen weak-stomached square heads. No, not half a dozen, just five, four with their heads over the side, one bent over talking to the deck with a towel over his head and shoulders, hidden. Suspicions began to reappear just as Bill set the bait. Arched her back, dropped the towel and looked up to the taller vessel. Just by chance, possibly, caught sight of Gino, split a wide and beaming smile.

"Hey big guy, you want a ride? Sun's burning the fuck out of me and these tight slope pricks won't go in till the boat's full."

With Nick bent over the side, Bill took advantage, added some emphasis, slapped hard across his arse.

"Won't listen to anything this weak prick tells 'em."

Small bikini, bouncing tits and the sound of an arse being bruised. Gino felt inspired. Bought out his charming best.

"You need a fucking man, woman."

Bill reeled him in.

"Sure do big guy, you know any?" With a happy thought he leapt aboard "I'll fuck this bitch in the boathouse". Stood tall to give her a good look.

While Gino flew, Tomas hit the full mixture, with air back in the engine it stirred back to health, the vessels drifted apart. No coming back now.

Hai hit the throttles, Gino hit the scuppers, hard on his right arm.

"Fucking slopes!"

Jerry plucked the pistol.

"You bastards, I'll fucking kill you!"

He rolled on his back to sit up, met four short barrels face to face. Lupras, peasant guns.

"Freeze shithead!"

Most of him froze, sphincter wobbled a bit.

Above the barrels, he recognised one of the faces. Skinny little prick, Nick, somehow always seemed to be leaving places whenever Gino arrived. They'd never met but Gino knew him by reputation, hard man but not a killer. Whether she knew it or not he figured that bitch was right, weak prick. Confidence reared its stupid head. He stared Nick in the face.

"What are you going to do, shoot me?"

Nick heard the scorn in his voice and thought, 'This dopey prick just makes things easier', before he replied.

"To tell the truth I will if I have to, but I'd really rather not. Too messy, have to waste an anchor to sink you and much too quick. Better you have some time to think while you're swimming."

His heart missed a beat, joy!

He'd watched the coast climb over the horizon a good five minutes before. The shoreline now not five miles distant. Kept his mouth shut while he congratulated himself. He could lay on his back and paddle from here, then there pricks would find out just what vengeance meant.

"I'll cut the bitch's teats off!"

He eased off his shoes as the boat rocked to a stop, unclipped the empty shoulder harness and slipped off his shirt. Took a good look at the faces aboard then turned and launched himself.

Bill let both barrels go, two barrels of salt, straight in the arse.

"That's from Robin!"

He screamed underwater, rolled in a ball and clenched at his bleeding buttocks.

For a moment Nick thought to pull him aboard, then thought what a silly thought that thought was.

"Don't go interfering with karma Nicky, he's got his chance, maybe he'll drown before the sharks get him."

Hai hit the throttles.

Nick gave directions.

"Put us on the beach, close to the pub, want people to see him leaving."

He threw hat and jacket at Jerry.

Heather had found a parking spot fifty metres from the pub.

What with the Watto considered the best public house this side of the city and Heather's more private house considered the same, many of the clientele visited both. She chose her disguise with careful thought, something way out of character, blatant and cheap, and something just for Jerry, something that screamed sex on legs. Chose a bright red Monaro to drive, just to add that suburban touch.

She stepped from the V8 as the boat hit the beach, heels just high enough to tense the calves, lots of legs, tiny hot pants with a yellow singlet that almost reached her navel, long black wig with a red beret.

Couple of people noticed.

Jerry stepped to the shore, turned and gave the bicep slapping fist-punching Italian salute, just in case they didn't understand he added the words "Fuck you."

Couple of more people noticed.

Heather cheap slut called and waved.

"Hey babe!"

Jerry did a double take, split his face with a grin so wide and deep Nick feared the back of the big fella's head might just fall off.

Gino/Jerry scampered up the street, swept the girl in his arms, into the V8 and gone, vroom vroom and disappeared in a cloud of smoke and lust.

More people noticed, though the small bag of guns went unseen. Two would return to their rightful owners, one would travel west. A trophy, proof of revenge for a sad, confused old Iman and his mad crippled son.

Except for the fun the new lovers enjoyed, the charade completely unnecessary. No one ever did come looking for Gino.

Nick slipped the brothers a monkey. They didn't want it.

"No phuck, no."

"Yes fuck, yes."

Couple of seasons as a union rep gave Nick a high regard for the value of labour, especially this kind.

"Yes, we're all good mates but nothing's for nothing. Take the money, buy Mama some flowers for me."

The brothers took the bills.

"She still want to see you."

"Soon as I can get there, see you guys, thanks."

While the boat pushed off and scooted back to Glebe, Nick led his three companions across the green, pointed a table.

"Grab a seat Bill and I'll get some drinks."

Tarik flicked an eyebrow.

"No worries mate, all good." Once alone with the girl he made comment.

"That was harsh."

The newly appointed Madam's voice showed a hard new edge.

"Harsh? You might have been prepared to give that prick a chance to come back, not me. Besides, wasn't it you who gave me a Sun Tzu to read? Strike hard where your enemy is soft and not looking. Sound familiar?"

Nick nodded in agreement.

"Yes mate, it does at that."

The service, as always was good, they strolled back in five minutes, a big jug of beer for three, a smaller jug of juice for their teetotal friend.

"What now?"

Nick grinned and replied.

"Well, if I was young and rich and good looking, like you guys seem to be, I'd sit right here and talk to some of the girls giving you the eye. Once Bill and I leave I reckon you two will start getting popular."

He turned to Lionel, and spoke to Tarik.

"I know he'll happily fuck anything on legs, how about you? You got anything against doing rude things to cute infidels?"

"How cute?" Tarik's companions shared a laugh. Nick slapped his shoulder.

"You'll fit right in son."

Lionel queried.

"What about you two?"

"Couple of beers, then I got some packing to do and a plane to catch."

He turned to Bill.

"Mind giving me a ride to the airport?"

"No problem."

Lionel queried some more.

"Haven't seen you for weeks, you back one day and gone again?" He smiled in reply.

"Getting old, mate, been a big day, could use a little seaside holiday."

HOME

AS THE LONG SWEEP hand rounded to the twelve mark, Nick struck the gong and called stop.

"Yame, change!" burst the Japanese word from his lips unconsciously, for years now part of his everyday lexicon.

Four of the eight training partners dropped the pads they were holding and helped their mates remove the gloves. Crammed into the timber deck, with the three bags hung down one edge, a heavy, a long and a triple floor to ceiling, it did not leave a lot of room to move around. Considering the fact most of their fights would be in crowded nightclubs, Nick's new/old back yard proved perfect for training, the home bar just inside the back door was popular too.

He did a quick double take to check what the other two hands on the old clock told him, muttered a quiet "Oh shit, here we go", and handed the mini mallet to Cyril.

"Give 'em three more rounds then stretch 'em. Let 'em cool right down then give 'em some grappling."
"Where you going?"
"Got Tiana coming."
"What? Bogadov's girl? The one Dave's going to marry? You bastard!"

"No! What? Get fucked, what kind of an arsehole you think I am?"

"Mate, ok, I know you're not an arse but you wouldn't have to be, that girl would make a blind monk horny."

"Yeah mate but it might be a bit embarrassing, Dave's coming with her."

"Of course he is. What are they? Joined at the hip? Never see him anymore unless she's standing next to him. Will not let that girl out of his sight."

"Would you? Smart too, four languages, top shelf education. Brought up on Soviet Naval bases."

"How the fuck he meet her?"

"Her old man. He was some kind of Russian Navy commander, retired. That thing in Moscow, thing they called 'Détente', in Georgia, that's where the good ones get to retire, they called it confusion, he took a chance, packed his family up and sailed here. You know that Militich, runs the game? He's a cousin of some sort. Anyway, he's invited the old man and gives her a job until she gets on her feet. Look good, smile at the players, keep cups and glasses full, see nothing, say nothing. She's good at all that. You should talk to her. Kev was standing next to Dave when she walked in. Reckons he was halfway through a sentence when he spotted her. Gob smacked him, stopped cold, mouth open, eyes sticking out of his head, stopped his silly shit in a heartbeat, took him two weeks to get back to what he was saying."

"What's he bringing her here for? Far as I know no one's ever got out of here without being fucked one way of the other?"

"My idea."

"What? You want her to start training?"

"No mate, information session."

"What?"

"Well, they're still pretty new in town, and every girl wants a fancy wedding, also a good excuse for the old man to say hello. He's happy to shell out for the whole thing, venue, food, music, wants a good show. She does too of course. Anyway, some of the jolly jokers at the game have been telling her silly stories about scary monsters showing up on Dave's side of the aisle. Thought it a good idea to get her around here for some introductions, take away some of the tension."

Gloves and pads exchanged, the fighters moved back to the deck as Nick rose and headed to the front door, listened to the tone of the torque-laden Thack! Thack! on the pads as the boys began a series of devastating leg kicks. He wandered up the hall of the two bedroom recently renovated cottage, briefly considered its history and continued out the front door, stepped past the narrow front garden and leant on the cast iron curly topped fence. With nowhere near the confidence he'd expressed to his one-time nurse and lifelong friend Cyril, he took the time to ask himself, "What the fuck am I going to say to this girl?"

Eyes narrowed in concentration, he drifted back into his own mind, searching for words that would give the would-be wife ease. Temporarily unemployed, his stilted vision wandered off across the street on its own. Stopped up against the front gate of one of two low-rise red brick apartment houses and struck a memory chord. A trick. Taught by an old chinaman, so long ago. Early in Nick's first visit to Woods Avenue. A useful trick, dismissive of pain and doubt, powerful too, a place where time, space and gravity held no sway.

He straightened. Opened his eyes wide and began the scan.

Not the familiar, that constant par favoured by forest watchers and posted guards alike, neglectful of detail but with antennae all abuzz searching for the thin wisps of smoke that portended bright red flame, for the movement and nuance in a crowded room that speak to the practised eye of imminent violence.

Not that one, the other.

One step at a time, the study of segments, the scavenge for detail.

The gate of number twelve slightly ajar, the curling edge or a dying brown leaf atop the bonnet of the eighty three silver Toyota parked twenty three and a half metres to the south. Detail.

Then beyond! Up the slope to the head of the avenue. The once imposing serf's entrance to a nineteenth century mogul's estate. Ten feet high, the hewn stone gateposts still stood, with overseers' houses adjacent, each an appropriate home for their imported professional residents, head groom to the west, head gardener to the east. To house their workers row cottages trailed behind. Six cottages this side then ornate stables, once twelve on the other, four now replaced by twin three-storey flats, right down to the street's abrupt ending, a block stone wall, eight feet high with paling fence atop.

Nick sucked in the sights, closed his eyes then started to drift.

Up.

Above the houses, over the power pole lines, one hundred, two hundred feet in the air, then turned and examined the results of a peat bog peasant's efforts. The teenage labourer had the temerity to insult his overseer. Strapped to the village triangle and flogged.

When the wounds healed, he located the bailiff who'd plied the whip.

Fourteen years transportation was the verdict for assault on the Crown's man. Due to the severity of the bailiff's injuries, the first six months in chains. The timing just right, his shackles removed on his second day in Sydney town.

Labour was not to be wasted in the fast growing colony, so, ticket of leave, serf to a colonist.

The corporal in charge considered his history, violence in response to command, and thought of a great entertainment, lease him to the lonely and detested jew, watch them tear each other apart. The great joke blew up in his face. A gentle and intelligent man, the lonely semite early on taught his charge to read, and later on kept the books for the canny and successful trader he became.

Trust grew, then wealth, then land. Land, that generation's long impossible dream to a peat bog peasant.

Of course, a lag could own nothing. Ten years of faith, while title deeds and profits grew in the nominal pockets of his mentor. Finally the long yearned freedom. Then the great test.

With no proof of his efforts and no rights at all, he looked to his long time master.

Isaac repaid his faith.

Meticulous books, profits astounding, land in abundance. Title deeds all stamped in the once felon's name. And then the great question. With freedom, and particularly with wealth, came choice. The ability to choose, to decide, to own his own life entire. Something he had never known. But what choice? What decision?

A triumphant return to Europe? To the cities?

Alternatively crowded or frozen streets, pestilent sewer-run lanes, a caste ridden world where wealth and intelligence, diligence and honesty, generosity and vision all counted for nought in the face of any degenerate blue bloodline.

Perhaps not the cities.

Back to his homeland?

Memories of fogs and bogs, of fen and swamp, the ever-menacing village triangle, starvation in winter and mothers' tears in the night.

Perhaps not.

Perhaps instead a fine Arab riding horse, perhaps mutton on a spit on the fallow land. Ale for the workers, music, a fiddler, perhaps even a jig.

His choice made itself.

Nick slipped through time, looked down the good man's legacy.

A generous repayment to the young country which had given him a life far beyond his, or his forebears' wildest dreams.

To the south, across that trunk road which linked the city hub to sandy coastline, Centennial Park, that jewel in the heart of the city's east. Twenty-seven rolling wooded acres, parks and ponds, ducks and flower beds, a gift to all.

To the east, two acres low-walled for a christian orphanage, fruit trees and chickens, even two goats, far from the foreboding workhouses of Europe. To the west, a synagogue grown on its own hectare.

To the north, the best of it all, the old Manor House now a near Saint's headquarters. Helen Keller. A comfortable home for the blind, deaf and dumb.

Expansive gardens, all heavily scented by the profusion of unseen flowers, surrounded by high hedge and fence.

The old stables long gone, a sturdy young oak in their place. For those who remembered, a special tree, two good men's bones beneath.

The avenue remained with one minor change, four cottages gone, two red brick constructions in their place.

A quiet buffered haven in the fast growing city.

So safe a haven, its fame found Mr Chen in far off Hong Kong. Not all that surprising, as chief unarmed combat instructor to the Hong Kong Military Police he found himself privy to much arcane information.

Japanese politics for instance.

The money came first. Four cottages dissolved, in their place grew red brick, twins almost to the family manse in the old British Hong Kong.

A timely man, he and his clan invested Woods Avenue as the Japanese Military invested Nanking.

From the sale of the bling the family brought in, worn openly or sewn in the clothing, a fish market stall soon followed, the restaurant not far behind. More years, a decade and plus.

More cottages became available, one side of the street entire.

Mr Chen sought a suitable neighbour. There was a man, an honest man, and already a neighbour, who owned a nearby stall at the markets. A seemingly delicate Cynthia Chen touched Fulvia on the elbow. Perhaps their fathers could speak?

More years, not many, he closed his eyes tighter, looked down on his own young self. Swathed in white. Memories flooded.

Fulvia's honeyed demands, heard vaguely next to his hospital bed. Angelo's shape by her side. She had soaked up the language and made her case well. With her law degree looming she had stated her well-thought points, always an impassioned debater, she had offered a level of attention nowhere available in the always crowded hospital system. The flame eyed, self appointed guardian would not accept rejection.

Her God had returned home, ashen and shaken, blood on his shirt, hole in his hat and a curious tale to tell. A boy! His saviour! This boy!

He was not going to die, just needed attention. While the Sisters of Mercy did give all their hearts, one nurse for ten patients was not the ratio she offered.

Ten passionate women, well versed in wound dressing, a dozen more star struck teenagers to keep a close watch, a doctor arm's length across the street.

That the doctor's degree was traditional Chinese she did not feel worthy of mention. Nor was it.

Then the celebrated homecoming, to a place he had never been.

Pills and pain and gentle ministrations, strange faces and scents and finally sense.

Awareness and shame, with both arms still bandaged and his chest still bound tight, an impossible task to wipe his own arse. Fulvia, of course, volunteered.

Nick's "NO" startled cats in the street.

Then Cyril. His father's son.

While still in high school, the money to pay for his doctor's degree had sat in the bank for ten years. His studies already intensive, three months as a practical nurse, with young sister Cynthia's watchful aid, was taken as great opportunity. Mr Chen thanked Nick, as Cyril wiped his bum.

A most curious start to a mutual respect, a unique beginning to friendship. Caused lots of laughs in the years to come. But first, there was healing. And education. For pain, for a short while, a long clumsy pipe, his arms both still quite useless, the stem fed to his lips by a gentle girl's fingers while Cyril took watch of his eyes. Just enough, not too much, not to slip into the opium stupor, some pain must remain, something to explore, something to investigate, something to manipulate.

"Hello pain, what's your name? Where do you live? Are you important right now? Are you important at all?"

Education began.

First Mr Chen, deep in his mind.

Then the Mothers, deep in his belly.

Raised as the victim of a stolid British kitchen, Nick's young palate had rarely known delight. As his pain became ignorable, his palate woke to wonder. With both arms still wrapped tight, for more than a month he needed hand feeding, small morsels brought to his lips.

Proud of their kitchens and proud of their duty, less than subtle competition began. Borscht and rich pastas for padding. They all had agreed, "the boy's much too thin."

Paella from Spain and schnitzels a la Salzburg. Rich rice-wrapped young prawns and Maltese calamari, whole red fish and sticky pork buns!

Then the sweet treats.

The tiny eclairs he almost inhaled, delicious! Sweet honey-soaked pastries, Baklava. And then came the cake, like nothing he'd ever eaten. From an old German recipe, so dark and rich someone apparently named a whole forest after it.

While Cyril was not terribly grateful for the near forced feeding, Nick didn't mind at all. He healed fast and strong, if just a little bit chubby.

Come the long waited day, bandages off!

A celebration was suggested. Everyone loves a party, and it seemed a good excuse. A day to be enjoyed, a day to be remembered.

Shirtless and pillow propped in Tony's armchair, outside the front door inside of the fence, Nick's long indoor skin soaked in the gentle winter sun. Could have been the vitamin D that made him grin, nature's happy pill, or perhaps the sight of the men at their labours. Trestles and chairs and long long lengths of wood, tables transported outdoors. One half a roof tile set under one leg, just to make all things even, then hastily away as the women took their turn.

Tablecloths and crockery, knives, forks and a table, then the first of the food, a rich Baltic stew, still simmering away in its big iron pot, be ready to eat in an hour.

Left plenty of time for debate.

Tony would brook no argument at table, so debates to be debated had best be debated before the eating got started.

An old circus tarp had been laid in the street. Mr Chen, by acclaim, had been appointed arbiter, his decisions would all go unchallenged. He would be quite busy for the next half hour so stepped across to talk to his children, silently. Nick had been blessed with two bookends the day he arrived, each with its designated duty.

Cynthia had the entry wound, Cyril, as with his other duties, the exit. With a shift of his eyes and a twist of his neck he explained to the kids their morning duty. The fence was quite strong, just a little bit short, and some coming debaters quite tall. Until debating was done and eating begun, the barrier must be defended.

Nick had been learning, saw what had been said, even caught the querily raised eyebrows. He'd wondered himself. Cyril had moved to his usual spot, Cynthia'd stood in his way; looked at his face; he moved to the left, an aberration, a change in an otherwise seamless pattern, the book end, reversed, why? The kids stood dead pan, 'nothing to see here'. Silent sibling conspiracy, what? Mr Chen knew his children, further questions at this point would be pointless. He turned to Fulvia to give verbal instruction, saw that would be pointless as well.

The blossoming woman had posted herself outside the gate, a short flensing knife clasped in her fist. She'd made her decision days before. Kicks, punches and head butts regardless, any man fool enough to stumble towards her charge would suffer a painful fate. Short sharp holes in the buttocks, she'd discovered, could move a man along quite quick.

Intense kind of woman.

The second debate had offered a clue to the kids' unusual posting.

Sam D'Agostini, number six, right next door, felt forced to defend his grappa. That silly great Pole from number eleven had declared his pear Schnapps the better.

The half dozen kids they owned between them pushed their way through knees and hips to gain a better view. With one exception. Young Tony seemed to prefer the view from the inside his own front fence. No more than an arm's length from Nick's right book end. He found the scents much better right there as well.

Sam had courage and speed, timing almost right as well. Two sharp lefts and a kick in shins, circle around to the right. The uppercut came quite unexpected. His arse hit the tarp and he rolled. Twin gasps of breath from Nick's near right, one in hopeful dismay 'Up Papa up!' One in hopeful sympathy.

Sam rolled, rolled again, back to his feet, knees bent, he felt the darkness coming on, so bent his knees a little bit further and pulled out a popular classic. Eternal favourite of fighting men everywhere, and spectators even more so.

The running, jumping, flying, diving, screaming head butt. Pauly dropped his chin to save his nose, caught him directly between the eyes. He staggered back, towards Nick's fence, stopped a short arm's length away.

Not far enough.

A short arm's length just right for a short arm to shoot out, close enough as well to hide the quick action from all but two sets of eyes.

Nick blinked, went dead pan, he liked that technique, he'd ask her about that one later.

Cyril's eyes flashed admonition, "you're going to get in trouble".

That particular sound he made, as the electric shock hit the back of brain and his arse hit the sandstone kerb, told Mr Chen exactly what had happened. Both fighters struggled gamely to their feet. Peter confused and impressed by the head butt's delayed effect, the small bruise inside his right elbow he'd never notice.

Mr Chen had called it a draw.

With the honour of their respective back yard distilleries successfully defended, the men threw arms about each other, one at the shoulder, one at the hip, and staggered together to the generous table.

Two more debates followed, neither venturing too far this side of the street. Nobody knew just what happened over there, but everyone did know there is no such thing as a time delay head butt.

Safer to fight over this side, Cynthia did seem a lot busier around the house for the next couple of months. Luckily, whenever her extra duties took her outside, that nice Italian boy across the street showed up to lend her a hand.

Nick grinned in reverie.

Mrs D'Agostini's apparently delicate arm stretched across the gap, touched Nick gently on the elbow.

"Visitors."

Nick snapped back to now.

The timing was just right, he had his answer, right in his face, like breathing, so taken for granted he hadn't seen it.

"Thanks, Cyn."

She smiled and waved as she turned indoors. Happy again now Nick was home. Far better than the previous tenant, that harlot.

Since their back fence screaming matches had ended the birds had returned to her garden, much nicer. With her own sons one year into their Navy enlistment and Tony forever at work, her home had grown quiet.

The new boys, in Nick's new back yard, laughter and sweat and young men competing. Brought life back into her days.

She'd sometimes slip around the back lane, since Tony installed the indoor plumbing, no longer the night soil collector's noxious passage, a jug of juice, a tray of sweet bites. She liked the new boys, bathed in their compliments. Good boys.

But still, tonight was her turn.

The extended family, still resident in her lifelong haven would all soon need feeding, and Tony home from the market. Cynthia's kitchen was her special delight, and twelve more cook books to sign and mail before the Post Office closed.

Busy busy, busy busy.

Nick smiled and slid his eyes from Cynthia's back to Tiana's front.

Silently cursed himself.

"Stop that!"

And then out loud.

"Hi guys, welcome, happy Friday."

Nick's customary welcome, quite cheery, changed every day, helped him remember as well, just when he was. Had a lot of fun had Nick, memory starting to suffer.

"Come through."

Opened the gate, led down his hall.

The old cottage had been remodelled while Nick took his break. The over feminine fripperies, scents, paint and gaudy art works all now just a bad memory for the stolid old brick.

New paint and bookcases, a wall mounted armoury, a stocked corner bar. A deck to cover the yard.

In the quiet of night you could hear the old place sigh.

Nick beckoned "Come out the yard, meet the boys."

He picked at her hesitation.

"Trust me girl, I used to sell used cars."

While Dave smiled at the cynicism, the culturally relevant joke went straight over the girl's head.

"Cars?"

Dave gave her hand a squeeze, even flashed Nick a hard look, just a little one.

"Don't worry darling, is nothing, just a silly Australian joke."

Nick turned, they followed. He thought, "She's smart, try her again on that one next year, see if she's been keeping her ears open, and her mind."

They stepped out onto the deck as Cyril called time.

"Heard some stories, some of the old boys at the game been teasing you, seems you expect scary monsters to show up on Dave's side of the aisle, madmen plus alcohol, that kind of the thing. Ruin your day.

Don't worry, that's not going to happen. I know that for true. Kevin and Yossi you already know, good blokes aren't they?"

"Good blokes?"

She considered the term.

"Yes, good blokes."

"Well girl, in this country, that's pretty much the best thing you can say about anyone. Man, woman or child, if you're a good bloke, just about everyone will to listen to what you have to say and give you a fair go."

"Now here's some more good blokes, have you met Lionel?"

"I have seen him, he visits Kevin sometimes."

The kiwi stepped up at the sound of his name, exchanged warm handshakes with this woman joining their lives.

"And when he visits, what kind of welcome does he get?"

"Oh, everybody loves Lionel."

"Not bad for a white skinned black fella grown up in an orphanage in New Zealand's biggest slum eh? True, he was a bit of a cranky bugger when he got here, but, just like everyone else, since he found a home he's calmed right down. Good bloke."

"Yes." She tried the unfamiliar term, "Good bloke".

"Now, don't expect you've met our man from Hong Kong."

He made introductions.

"Cyril, Tiana, Tiana, Cyril."

Cyril clasped his right fist in his left hand at a chest height, nodded a small bow.

Nick was impressed when she mirrored his action.

Thought "no arrogance, polite, beginning to like this girl."

Then Cyril added his bit.

"Don't listen to that man from Hong Kong shit, I was born in that block across the street."

Nick leapt to his own defence.

"Poetic licence, me old son. Thing is, why you were born in that block across the street. Family was doing pretty well in China wasn't it?"

"Same as everyone else, war. Dad was working with the police. He was the first one they were going to shoot."

"Better here?"

"Bloody good here mate! Bloody Japs." He swivelled and glared theatrically at his sticky hands training partner.

Nick turned back to Tiana, with a small in-house grin.

"Speaking about sons of Nippon, have you met Fuji?"

The Filipino stepped forward with straight backed formality.

"Thank you for your invitation, may your sons be strong and your daughters as beautiful as their mother."

Nick broke in.

"Well listen to you, Mr Honey Tongue, how about telling her why you're not still in Manila?"

Fuji struggled, "Same as everyone, war. When the last big one ended Japanese weren't real popular in the Philippines. Lots of violence."

Nick neglected to mention the worst of the violence had come from Fuji's father's Tommy gun collection. Still, if you back a tiger into a corner things are always going to end bloody.

"Better here?"

Fuji smiled as he stepped away.

"Just a bit."

"Stevie."

The two-metre Tongan glided towards the small tight group. Dave tensed just that tiny bit.

"Look at that fucker. Smooth as cat shit on ice."

Nick noticed the envy. It had taken Dave months to achieve that fluidity, the big hearted Baptist minister had picked it up in a week.

His wide toothed grin faded the afternoon sun as he wrapped her hands in his.

"So very pleased to meet you, miss, thank you for inviting me."

His high pitched sweet voice surprised her, she'd been expecting something more like the roar of a bear.

Nick asked.

"How about you tell Tiana how come you're here? Tonga's beautiful isn't it?"

Stevie answered sadly.

"Nowhere to stand anymore. I have eight brothers and five sisters, and now there is surf where our village use to be. Every year, more people, less land. We had to come to the big island."

Nick saw it a little differently, his thought slipped out.

"That's the worst war, the rich against the earth. That one will never end."

"War?"

"It never ends, it never changes. Wherever there is life there is conflict. Wherever there are men there are greed and lust for power. Powerful nations use the weak, ten million Chinese buy refrigerators, five million yanks buy v-eights. Stevie's island home sinks into the sea. The young hate the old ways, the old fight changes, Christian hates Jew hates Muslim hates Christian. All sad, painful, wasteful rubbish. All usually directed by princes, priests and self-serving politicians.

Nobody flees a happy home. The smart ones who do, they come here. We're too young a nation for princes and by the time we get here, too well educated, wounded, to listen to maniac priests who talk directly to God. Everyone here has a bruise in their heart, that's what makes them worth knowing. Until you've known pain you know nothing."

"And here's another of our clever little group, Jerry, Tiana, Tiana, Jerry."

She had heard of Jerry, and his nickname "Mr Invisible", he was not what she expected.

Six and a half feet from the ground, a bright baldy head, shoulders from here to way over there.

They shook.

"Pleased to meet you at last. Thank you for your invitation. I will be there."

Something there suggested she might not see him, but he will be there. He spoke in a broad pommie accent.

"How about telling Tiana why you're here. Where you're from."

"Same as everyone else, war of one sought or another. Mine was black against white. Brixton. If you're black you join a gang as soon as you can, same thing if you're white. Saves you getting kicked to death on your own. Mum got out, I joined the army, safer there. Finished that, then they let me come."

"Better here?"

"Fuck yeah, make my own choices, who to hate, who to love."

Nick smiled, six months before he'd not have added that last bit. Life with Heather must be good. Especially now she's out of the game.

Jerry stepped off, then came Nick's worry. Bill.

He worried how this would go, women. He'd long ago learned he had no idea. Both of them smart, both of them strong, both with their own opinions. This could go either way.

Bill lurched forward, just a bit eager. Embraced the smaller woman. Her right eye swept a little, washed over Dave. Tiana's left eye followed.

Nick gasped, quietly.

"Did they titter? Like schoolgirls giggle?"

He had no idea. Tiana'd won Bill the day the news, as it always does, filtered through.

The day she had Dave drive her about the town with a leather bag, full cardboard boxes, full of rolex wrist watches, and small notes of apology.

Great fan of clean starts, Tiana.

They peeled apart, future meetings sure to follow. Nick began to feel just that little bit sorry for Dave. With two of them together he was hopelessly outnumbered.

Threw that thought aside as she introduced the last of today's backyard crew.

"And last, but not least, our man from Babylon, Tiana, Tarik, Tarik, Tiana."

Tiana hesitated.

"Babylon?"

"May as well be, no one knows where he was from but he could speak six languages by the time he was eight. And now he's got English."

Tiana offered a hand.

Tarik gave a deep salaam straightened and shook the surprised girl's hand.

Tiana blanched.

"Islam?"

Nick draped an arm across the square shoulders of his new friend.

"Doesn't drink, does not tell lies, knows exactly what's being said in any language you're liable to hear in the Cross and would rather cut his own hand off than steal from the till. Can you think of anyone better to sell alcohol to infidels?"

Tiana smiled, ventured to ask.

"How did you come here?"

Tarik smiled, in memory, the days he recalled now had one wonderful fact. They were over.

"There was a house, then the tents, then everybody was dead, then the army in Turkey, then Victor found me. My uncle, the last of my blood".

"My wedding, a synagogue?"

There is one God, he is everywhere, I will be with you and he will be with me."

The proud young Muslim salaamed again and stepped away.

Nick offered the comment he'd been waiting to make.

"You know anything about steel?"

"I studied marine engineering, in Stalingrad."

"I know steel."

The kind of reply a serious, well-educated young engineer might make, one which left little wriggle room. A wall of certainty.

Nick slipped through an unexpected gap.

"Then you know you don't make it out of iron?"

"Yes, you do."

"No you don't. If you want good steel, the best kind, you need dirt as well. You need clay and carbon. You need heat and pressure. You meld it and mix it, heat it and bend it, then beat it real hard. Then heat it again and mix it, then bend it again and beat it again. And again and again. And then cool it, that's very important, and shape it, and polish it fine. Bring out the beauty that lives inside."

Tiana smiled as he spoke, beginning to see the point he was trying to make, the story sat comfortable in her belly, something she understood, and agreed with.

"Same thing with countries, same thing with people. Place that's happening most nowadays is my country, our country, and now your country.

Everyone in this yard has been heated and beaten on. Don't worry, that's what you're going to get on Dave's side of the aisle darling, Australians. We come from cities and towns and deserts and swamps all over the world.

For some, depending how deep the swamp they come from, it can take a generation to get the mud out of their ears, but in the end everyone gets the idea. There's nothing to stop you choosing to be a good bloke. Some of these buggers might not look real pretty on the outside but everyone one of 'em's got something better than good on the inside. You're going to marry one of ours, so we already love you. Once you get to know us I am sure you'll start loving us back."

A very pretty woman bent forward and kissed Nick on the check.

He stayed happy right up until the moment the front door called.

"Phuck!!"

Lightning Source UK Ltd.
Milton Keynes UK
UKOW06f2336130616

276264UK00020B/406/P